Happy retirement?

The impact of employers' policies and practice on the process of retirement

Sarah Vickerstaff, John Baldock, Jennifer Cox and Linda Keen

First published in Great Britain in July 2004 by

The Policy Press
Fourth Floor, Beacon House
Queen's Road
Bristol BS8 1QU
UK

Tel no +44 (0)117 331 4054
Fax no +44 (0)117 331 4093
E-mail tpp-info@bristol.ac.uk
www.policypress.org.uk

© University of Kent 2004

Published for the Joseph Rowntree Foundation by The Policy Press

ISBN 1 86134 584 4

British Library Cataloguing in Publication Data
A catalogue record for this report is available from the British Library.

Library of Congress Cataloging-in-Publication Data
A catalog record for this report has been requested.

Sarah Vickerstaff is Reader in Employment Policy and Practice, **John Baldock** is Professor of Social Policy, **Jennifer Cox** was Research Associate on the research project and **Linda Keen** is Honorary Senior Research Fellow, all at the School of Social Policy, Sociology and Social Research at the University of Kent.

The **Joseph Rowntree Foundation** has supported this project as part of its programme of research and innovative development projects, which it hopes will be of value to policy makers, practitioners and service users. The facts presented and views expressed in this report are, however, those of the authors and not necessarily those of the Foundation.

Cover design by Qube Design Associates, Bristol
Printed in Great Britain by Hobbs the Printers Ltd, Southampton

Contents

Acknowledgements

We would like to thank the Joseph Rowntree
Foundation for their sponsorship of this research
as part of its 'Transitions after 50' research
initiative. For encouragement, helpful comments
on draft material and stimulating discussion we
would like to thank members of our project
advisory group (Mark Hinman, David Bryan,
Michelle Lewis and Richard Scase) and especially
Donald Hirsch, the Programme Adviser. Special
thanks are also due to the three organisations
that so generously opened their doors to us and
to the many individuals who agreed to be
interviewed.

The responsibility for the content and
conclusions of the report rests, as ever, solely
with the authors.

Executive summary

There is widespread anxiety about current patterns of retirement:

- the tendency for the average length of the working life to decrease;
- individual worry about the likely value of occupational and/or state pensions; and
- government concern about the ageing workforce and the worsening of the dependency ratio.

It is in this context that extending the average working life has come centre stage of many policy discussions (see, for example, House of Lords, 2003). The argument here is that any attempt by government to influence or stem the tide of early retirement will need to focus as much on employers' management of human resources as on individual motivations and the impacts of social policy. This report focuses on this previously neglected area: employers' policies and practice as a dynamic force in retirement decisions. The research detailed here involved interviews with managers and a total of 160 employees and ex-employees in three case study organisations. The interviews covered:

- the organisations' policies with regard to retirement and pensions;
- individuals' knowledge and understanding of their organisation's approach to retirement issues;
- individuals' retirement aspirations, plans and activities in retirement; and
- attitudes to the idea of downshifting workload prior to full retirement.

The key findings are as follows.

- There are lost opportunities, inefficiencies and inequalities in the way that the retirement process is currently managed.
- A lack of knowledge and understanding of pension policies and retirement options seriously undermines many people's capacity to plan ahead for retirement.
- Most people would welcome more choice about when to retire.
- Individuals and organisations are motivated to explore the possibilities for downshifting work roles prior to retirement but the impact on pension entitlement presents a significant barrier.

Introduction

In this report we address a neglected area of research into retirement and older workers: the employing organisation. Most research has concentrated on four main areas: first, mapping demographic trends in labour force participation rates of older age groups and their implications (for example, Gregg and Wadsworth, 1998; Campbell, 1999; Alcock et al, 2003); second, typically using longitudinal data, modelling correlations between a range of individual difference variables such as paid employment, income levels, health, marital status, presence or absence of an occupational pension and retirement (Disney et al, 1997; Meghir and Whitehouse, 1997; Tanner, 1998; Bardasi et al, 2000; Bardasi and Jenkins, 2002; DWP, 2003); third, traditional social policy analyses of the genesis, development and modification of state pension policies (for example, Bonoli, 2000), their differential impact on various groups, for example on women (Ginn et al, 2001; Evason and Spence, 2003), and the problems of non-take-up of benefit entitlement among pensioners (for example, Evason et al, 2002). Lastly, social gerontologists have concentrated on the consequences for self and identity and for families and social networks rather than on the retirement decision itself.

These various strands of research have not focused on the employing organisation's policy and practice as a dynamic force in retirement decisions. As Beehr (1986, pp 45-6) commented as a result of the first two strands of research on individual difference variables we derive "knowledge about the 'causes' of retirement decisions [which] is more correctly labelled knowledge about 'predictors' of retirement decisions". As a result of the third and fourth strands of research we understand some of the dynamics behind policy change in the pension

field and its effects in terms of the likelihood and experience of poverty in older age. However, there remain considerable gaps in what might be called 'the theory of the retirement transition'. To what extent is retirement an individual choice or decision and to what extent is it merely reactive and constrained by the decisions of employing organisations, the rules of occupational pension entitlement and redundancy schemes? This report begins the task of bringing the organisation back into the study of retirement processes by researching the impact of employers' age management policies and practices on retirement decisions.

Brief description of the study

The main aims of the research reported here were to:

- examine how older workers and the retirement process are currently managed in a range of organisations;
- identify barriers to effective planning for retirement;
- consider whether individuals feel there is enough choice when facing decisions about retirement;
- evaluate from both the employers' and individuals' viewpoints the potential merits of 'flexible retirement' – that is, the ability for individuals to downshift or reduce work commitments in the run up to full retirement.

To this end the research involved a series of organisational case studies that situate the individual's decisions and experience in the context of the employer's age management policies. A qualitative research methodology was chosen as the best way to explore the variety and complexity of individual experience. Such research cannot be generalised in the manner of statistical or numerical surveys but it can provide critical insights into "how things work in particular contexts" (Mason, 2002, p 1). It can also reveal connections between factors hitherto not linked and generate hypotheses for larger samples to test. As the focus of the research questions was on the management of the retirement process it was appropriate to undertake case studies based within particular organisations. This allowed individual employee descriptions and accounts of events to be placed alongside policy documents and managerial records of the same processes. A multiple case-study approach (looking at three different organisations) provided the opportunity for comparison of the effects of different policy regimes and managerial practices (Bryman, 2001, pp 51-4). Thus, the organisations were chosen to represent different sectors and workforce profiles (see 'Case study organisations' box, below).

Case study organisations

Case 1: LOCALGOV The first case study organisation is in local government. This serves as a critical case as the sector has a recent past history of considerable early retirement.

Case 2: TRANSPORT The second organisation is a private sector organisation in the transport industry with a large manual and routine white-collar workforce. The organisation is in a fiercely competitive and turbulent industry.

Case 3: HEALTH PRODUCTS The last organisation is a multinational research-based company in medicines and health products with a large, highly educated professional and managerial staff.

All three organisations are based in the south of England; however, they recruit from both buoyant and depressed labour markets. Permanent employees in all of the organisations have access to an occupational pension scheme and thus are part of the 37% of the population fortunate enough to benefit from such schemes.

In addition to interviewing human resource and pensions managers and trade union representatives in the organisations, the main body of the research involved semi-structured interviews with 160 individuals. These respondents were from three points in the retirement process: employees in their forties and fifties who have not yet seriously considered retirement, employees approaching retirement, and those who had retired from the organisation in the last five years (see the Appendix for further details). In order to ensure the anonymity of interviewees, when interviews are quoted directly in the report, in the case of employees or the retired, respondents are identified by their interviewee number, their work status and their organisation, and in the case of managers or trade union representatives by their job title and organisation.

A note on the meaning of 'retired'

Blaikie reminds us that "retirement is a decidedly malleable concept" (1997, p 11). This research and the work of others demonstrate that many people who take early retirement from one employer continue to seek and find paid employment in the labour market (Dench and Norton, 1996; Phillipson, 2002). Writers in the field have commonly drawn a distinction between 'retirement' and 'early exit', the former referring to reaching the state's pension age, the latter to the point at which older workers make an early exit from permanent paid employment (for example see Kohli and Rein, 1991, pp 5-6; Lissenburgh and Smeaton, 2003). Guillemard talks of "definitive withdrawal from the labour market" (1997) to distinguish between those who are not working and do not intend to in the future (the 'fully' retired) and those who leave organisations well in advance of normal retirement ages and spend some years moving between the statuses of economically active and inactive. In this study, because our starting point is the employing organisation from which someone retires, our respondents are designated as 'retired' if they have officially retired from the case study organisation. This does not, of course, mean either that they have reached the state pension age or that they are currently not in paid employment.

Structure of the report

The findings of the research are broken down into four sections as follows: the nature and practice of employer policies; employee and retiree understanding of policy and pensions;

individuals' experience and desire for choice
over when and how to retire; and, lastly,
attitudes to downshifting. A concluding section
provides summaries of the findings and seeks to
draw out the policy implications of these.

2

The management of older workers and retirement

The issues of recruitment, retention, utilisation, deployment and early labour market withdrawal of older workers are currently high on political agendas as the government seeks to encourage people to work for longer and delay their retirement. Research reveals that the majority of people who cease to work in their fifties do not choose to do so (Campbell, 1999; Hayden et al, 1999; PIU, 2000; Arthur, 2003). They leave their jobs through redundancy, early retirement or ill-health. However, relatively little research on employer practice in these areas has been undertaken recently (DfEE, 2000, p 11). Hence it is vital to explore the management practices that underpin the management of older workers and retirement. In this chapter we consider these issues under three headings. We start by looking at the pension and retirement policies that the case study organisations had in place. Next we look at how these policies were applied in practice. Finally, we consider the extent to which the case study organisations have changed, or were changing, their policies in these areas and what the context for these developments was.

Retirement and pension policies

Permanent employees in all three organisations have access to an occupational pension scheme (see pension arrangements box) and all three organisations provided for early and ill-health retirements. LOCALGOV and HEALTH PRODUCTS also had provisions for early retirement on grounds of efficiency. Employees in all organisations can request early retirement with abated pension from the age of 50. The decision is at management's discretion.

From April 1998 the regulations for the Local Government Pension Scheme were modified and each individual local authority has discretion over the enhancements they might offer for early retirement and is required to have a published policy. In LOCALGOV and other parts of local government there is also the 85-year rule, namely that if your years of service and your age add up to 85 then you can retire with a full pension. However, management still has discretion over the final decision for those who satisfy the rule but are not yet 60. The National Employers' Organisation for local government is currently investigating ways of abolishing the 85-year rule.

The situation in TRANSPORT was more complicated and undergoing considerable change during the course of the research. Three pension schemes were in operation in TRANSPORT for different groups of employees; two of these were national sector-wide schemes and the third was a company pension. They each had different retirement ages, 61 and 62 for the national schemes and 63 for the company scheme. These had been the ages at which employees were required to retire until modifications introduced very recently in which there was now some scope for people to carry on working to the age of 65. Some employees prior to this change also had retirement dates of 65 because they were working under different contracts originally drawn up in another company that was merged with TRANSPORT.

In LOCALGOV and HEALTH PRODUCTS there is considerable management discretion over the operation of retirement provisions. In TRANSPORT management's hand is much more driven by the terms of the different pension schemes. Despite this difference, interviews with managers, employees and retirees in all of the

Pension arrangements

LOCALGOV
The Local Government Pension Scheme is a statutory, contributory final salary scheme. Thus, the level of salary and number of years' service in the scheme determine the level of pension. The normal retirement age for all Local Government Pension Scheme members is 65.

TRANSPORT
There are three pensions in operation:
* Senior Staff Pension Fund, a national industry-wide contributory final salary scheme, under which the normal pension age is 61.
* Routine Staff Pension Plan, a national industry-wide contributory defined benefit scheme until 2001; thereafter a defined contribution or money purchase scheme. Under both, normal retirement age is 62.
* Company Pension Scheme – prior to a merger with another company the company pension had been a contributory defined benefit scheme, with a normal retirement age of 63. The merger company had a defined contribution scheme with a normal retirement date of 65. The new group pension scheme is a defined contribution scheme with a normal retirement age of 63.

HEALTH PRODUCTS
The Company Pension Scheme is a non-contributory final salary scheme. The normal retirement age is 65.

organisations revealed some ambivalence over the relative roles of the organisation's management and the pension fund trustees in making decisions about early retirement and retirement ages.

"Retirement decisions are if anybody wanted to take early retirement, which they can request from being 50, then the request has to come via their HR manager and then we sort of endorse whether it's going to be possible to allow their retirement to go ahead. The ultimate decision though is made by the pension trustees because obviously the earlier someone retires the longer they're going to receive their pensions so it is their ultimate decision but I would think at that stage if the manager says its OK and HR says it's OK to release they would only ask sort of questions about will I be taking a pension so they can get another job outside or what the situation is." (Senior HR advisor 1, HEALTH PRODUCTS)

"Well, they don't have any real influence on what I want to do or not. I mean my retirement is governed by the [National Scheme]. I just happen to work for [TRANSPORT]." (R106, male manual employee)

Even with the company schemes in HEALTH PRODUCTS and TRANSPORT, pensions were practically and physically organised separately from the human resources management (HRM) function. Among HR professionals in all three organisations there was a sense that pensions were complicated, difficult and largely the responsibility of the 'pension specialists'. They were not seen as a part of mainstream HRM, although its significance for the effective management of human resources was recognised:

"So there are quite a large number of people with a lot of experience who are all sort of starting to reach retirement age and I think it's probably time that we started to think about that in a bit more of a systematic way because we potentially are losing a huge knowledge base from the organisation." (Senior HR policy advisor 2, HEALTH PRODUCTS)

"So in a way I suppose we're not active in sort of promoting the pension arrangements or the facilities that people have got to make good pension arrangements here … as pensions become an ever higher profile issue in employment terms at the moment we're holding our own … we can still say we offer a final salary pension scheme and there are increasing number of firms who don't." (Senior personnel advisor, LOCALGOV)

"You can put a lot of effort into the package to entice people in but actually managing the career and then the exit is quite crucial." (Strategic director, LOCALGOV)

Some of the difficulties organisations experience in managing their pension provision may arise from the prevailing regulations about what advice and information employers are allowed to give employees (DWP, 2004, p 223). As in other areas where employment relations are legally regulated (for example equal opportunities) a lack of clear understanding of the implications of rules can lead employers to be overcautious in their response. The recent Department for Work and Pensions white paper proposes a number of measures to clarify the employers' role in giving and promoting pension information (DWP, 2004, p 23).

The management of retirement: the application of policies

Final decisions about retirement are still largely at the discretion of the employing organisation. This discretion and the complexity of provisions for different groups was felt by many respondents (both managers and employees) to be used in an apparently arbitrary way, so that some people struck lucky and were offered deals or were allowed to go while others in similar circumstances were not.

"I mean we have just been dealing with a high level grievance relating to that in terms of someone saying I'm meeting the 85-year rule, I want to go and essentially their grievance is I've seen other people benefit from this in the past, I want a bit of the same please and we're saying well no, things have changed I'm afraid. And again there is a significant cost there. Even two years before the age of 60 there is something like £25K that it's going to cost the organisation to do that and that money will just simply be handed over to the pension fund and we're saying we're not minded to do that." (Senior personnel advisor, LOCALGOV)

"This is where they went completely wrong. We had to go up to [X] County Cricket Ground, all of us ... and the LOCALGOV [S] as he then was said he was looking for people to take early retirement and we were encouraged to put our names forward from a certain age and the deal they were offering was very good. So I put my name forward and I didn't get it and I did that two or three times." (R50, female ex-secretary retired, LOCALGOV)

"They offered this enhancement a few years ago which was probably a way anyone over 50 I think it was, would get a five years enhancement which I suppose they would qualify for. There are a lot of people hoping they'll do it again but...." (R165, male employed manual worker, HEALTH PRODUCTS)

LOCALGOV's approach to early retirement and the pension scheme, like many other public and private sector employers, had been largely tactical in the past. Pressure to change approaches to retirement in local government came from outside, primarily from the criticisms contained in the Audit Commission's report *Retiring nature* in 1997. HEALTH PRODUCTS took the view that as it offered a very generous non-contributory pension scheme, its general intention was not to offer enhanced pensions as a way of reducing headcount, although it too had done so in the past. Requests from employees in HEALTH PRODUCTS to take early retirement with reduced years' pension entitlement were typically accepted; no one could provide an example of a case where it had been refused. In TRANSPORT, for those employees pensioned under national sector schemes, there was no scope for the direct employer to enhance pension entitlement.

Nevertheless, employing organisations are reluctant to lose entirely the flexibility to offer early retirement as a means of reducing headcount or shifting particular employees. This discretion can work both ways:

"I would retire this year if the organisation would let me retire. As you know with local government you can retire at any time onwards from 50 but between 50 and 60 it has to be with management permission before you can actually draw your pension.

So I'm at the stage at the moment of saying I would like to retire and the organisation is at the stage of saying we want you to stay. So there's nothing unpleasant or awkward about it but that's the stage we've got to at the moment." (R20, male employed manager, LOCALGOV)

"I've noticed in the past in libraries the opportunity to see some people leave if that's been presented them they've taken it and for the sake of refreshing managerial posts or whatever. So I think it has been a tool in the weaponry of the [LOCALGOV] Council for refreshing." (R51, male employed manager, LOCALGOV)

The use of this managerial discretion tactically, that is in an ad hoc way to meet pressures arising from other organisational or business demands, can of course result in perverse longer-term consequences:

"So it is about managing individuals' expectations around that [prospects for early retirement]. I think really we've done quite well as an organisation in recent years in terms of saying the costs are so great it's just not going to happen. The problem is from time to time it's convenient for the organisation to allow it to happen so then we shoot ourselves in the foot as an organisation when we do allow individuals the package to go because it solves an organisational problem and other people say well I've seen that happening over there, can I have the same? And we're saying so in effect if you're a problem bizarrely you can get rewarded, or the perception is you can get rewarded being so ... and here's your money sort of thing." (Senior personnel advisor, LOCALGOV)

However, organisations can also deploy other policies to encourage people to 'opt' for retirement, as the following quotations demonstrate:

"I mean there are instances where people are given financial incentives but in two instances that I am particularly thinking of at this time there were no financial incentives given. It was a case of well you've both done over 30 years service, your pensions are quite healthy and these

jobs are no longer in existence within the framework of this laboratory.

"If you don't want to go we will put you into jobs in other departments, not necessarily ones that you want to do but that's what's going to happen if you don't take retirement." (R175, male employed technician, HEALTH PRODUCTS)

"I really never considered it [retirement]!... And I got quite a big payout you see, to go.... I mean the post was deleted from the establishment. And it would have meant taking something lesser.... Post deleted and involving taking a lesser job, which psychologically isn't very good. Working with the same team.... I think it's psychologically not good for the team or anything else if you're going to do a job that is lesser – um – you know and er – one felt well there's other things out there [laughs] don't hang around." (R1, female white-collar retired, LOCALGOV)

If the application of policies on early retirement appears somewhat arbitrary and difficult for the individual to predict, in other instances the application of fixed normal retirement ages is felt to be too rigid:

"Well that really wasn't a decision on my part at all. It's [TRANSPORT] policy to retire you at 61 and in actual fact I would have liked to have stayed because I was on a good wage and I would have liked to have stayed on perhaps another two or three years although I was getting a bit worn out and stressed and everything but I would have liked to have had that full pay for a little bit longer before I retired but I had no choice." (R61, male white-collar worker retired, TRANSPORT)

"I've got to retire.... Where I like it or lump it."

"Right. So it's the company retirement age?"

"Yes. I don't feel old enough do I? I mean I can get away with not being 65 at the moment." (R144, male employed manual worker, HEALTH PRODUCTS)

However, here again organisations had discretion to allow people to continue working beyond normal retirement age. In LOCALGOV this was not uncommon and was typically a matter for local discretion in the service concerned. In HEALTH PRODUCTS no one could think of any examples other than where those who had retired early might be re-employed on a consultancy basis in their area of specialism. In TRANSPORT there was a major policy change during the course of the research to allow employees to work beyond the normal retirement age where there was work available for them to do. They were to be re-employed on a different contract. This modification to policy was so new that many respondents had been interviewed before the policy change, and word about it had not reached everyone who was interviewed subsequently.

Policy changes

We are in a period of considerable flux in company policy on early retirement, retirement and pension provision at the present time. Public sector employers, following criticism from the Audit Commission and others, have been seeking to reduce the numbers taking early retirement and ill-health retirement and their performance is now subject to wider public scrutiny through the requirement to publish Best Value Performance Indicators in these areas. Many large private organisations have recently abandoned or significantly modified their final salary pension schemes, with a shift to defined contribution or money purchase schemes, because of fears of the rising costs of pensions as people retire earlier and live longer. All three of our case study organisations were experiencing some changes to existing policies, most notably in LOCALGOV and TRANSPORT.

Employers now risk higher costs if they use early retirement as a business management tool. Revisions to the Local Government Pension Scheme Regulations in 1997 (with effect from 1998) transferred the costs of early retirement to the employing organisation. The Audit Commission report recommended that employers bear the full costs of early retirement decisions and in LOCALGOV it was implemented by making the individual service directorates responsible for funding any early retirements from their revenue budgets. This had the immediate effect of making the costs of early retirement with enhanced pension transparent and part of service directors' immediate cost considerations. Personnel managers universally saw this 'devolution' of responsibility as having concentrated the minds of managers.

> "When they started to see individual cases and let's say the cost was 85,000 for this case it started to focus the mind a wee bit [laughs]!... And I think it rather horrified people to see how much it cost for someone to retire early.... I mean we have had individual cases where the cost has been in excess of half a million." (Senior manager, LOCALGOV)

As a result, policy and practice are changing in LOCALGOV. As well as reducing the number of early retirements there is an overall move to integrate retirement and pension issues into a new reward strategy (Vickerstaff et al, 2003, p 277).

In relation to stemming the tide of early and ill-health retirements, the approach by LOCALGOV has been led more by practice than formal changes of policy:

"Is it difficult to turn the culture of early retirement around?"

> "If you'd asked me this question a year ago I'd have said yes, but we just did it, and didn't make a big song and dance about it. As cases came up – and some of them were pretty high profile – it was made quite clear that actually we were not in the market of retiring people early. If they were on fixed-term contracts we were in the market for renewing them, not for ending them and paying them. A number of quite senior figures were 'got' that way. The Chief Executive personally for example had filtered that message through – the Directors the same – saying, 'This is nonsense for us to spend a quarter of a million getting rid of someone that we have to replace, and we don't really want them to go anyway'. So we just for the last year have been very very rigorous on this, we've really only allowed let go people we wanted to." (Strategic director, LOCALGOV)

Figure 1: Management discretion in the retirement zone

AGE	EARLY RETIREMENT ZONE FROM 50	COMPANY'S NRA	POST NRA
AREA OF MANAGEMENT DISCRETION OVER RETIREMENT CHOICE	Accept employee's request Employer triggers for business reasons Employer triggers for other reasons (eg ill-health, redundant skills)	Employer policy for workers to retire at given age Illegal from 2006	Allow employees to continue on same contract Offer different contract or consultancy

LOCALGOV has managed to restructure expectations about early retirement (with enhanced pensions) in quite a short time, although organisational rumours and myths about what those at the top can negotiate for themselves persist. A trade union representative confirmed that people's perceptions were generally that early retirement was now more difficult to get but that as a result the union was dealing with more petitions for ill-health retirement.

In TRANSPORT there was a policy change during the course of the research, the full implications of which were not yet apparent. There were moves to allow employees to continue working beyond the normal retirement ages under the prevailing pension rules, if suitable work was available for them. The pension schemes available for TRANSPORT workers had also gone through periods of change (see pension arrangements box, p 5). The national sector schemes had undergone modification under financial pressures and the company pension had to accommodate commercial mergers and acquisitions with other companies. This had resulted in some outcomes that individual employees felt were perverse. In particular the national senior staff scheme had had the facility for members to retire at 57 on a full pension – that is, with four years' pension enhancement. This opportunity had ended in 2000, with the result that a number of those interviewed had by dint of their ages either benefited or not. Once again the effect of these changes both in company and pension scheme policy was to reduce people's expectations of early retirement.

HEALTH PRODUCTS' employees were divided about the retirement culture in their organisation. Some felt that there was no particular pressure to go early or to stay until normal retirement age; it was largely a matter for individual decision and negotiation. Others felt strongly that HEALTH PRODUCTS was a 'young company' and that there was an expectation that people would go before the normal retirement age, although there was in most cases no overt pressure to do so. The average age at retirement for the retired respondents from HEALTH PRODUCTS was marginally lower than for the other two organisations but predicted retirement ages among the still-employed were very similar across all three organisations. There was a general feeling that the company would probably not offer enhanced early retirement deals in the future, a fact lamented by some.

A recent acquisition of another company by HEALTH PRODUCTS had raised issues in employees' minds about how the pension scheme of the other organisation would be integrated with the HEALTH PRODUCTS pension. Respondents in all three organisations were aware of the current turbulence in pension policies and the number of employers moving away from final salary schemes. However, overall employees in LOCALGOV and HEALTH PRODUCTS expressed confidence in their pensions and believed that they would continue to enjoy final salary schemes. It is not possible to generalise on the basis of our three cases but there is certainly evidence here that these employees felt that the era of early retirement with enhanced pensions had gone.

Summary

Figure 1 illustrates that as employees enter the retirement zone, typically from 50 years of age, there are a range of options: early retirement, retirement at the 'normal age' or continuing to work beyond the normal retirement age (NRA). A decision about actual retirement at any of these points is at management's or the pension funds' discretion. The individual may request early retirement but be turned down, they may ask to continue working after normal retirement age but be denied, they may work alongside other employees who conversely do retire early or are allowed to carry on working or come back on a consultancy basis to undertake projects for the organisation. The exercise of discretion puts a premium on how organisations manage their older workers and the retirement process by highlighting potential inequalities between individuals.

In the light of upcoming legislation on age discrimination in 2006 it may be that organisations operating in this way will find it difficult to provide adequate rationales or justifications for why one individual was allowed to do something that another was not if the individual can make a case that age, rather than any assessment of performance, was the deciding factor.

The picture that emerges from the case study companies is that the management of older workers, retirement and their pensions were not accorded any strategic significance in their own right; what happened here was derived from other, often unrelated, policy pressures. This echoes the findings of research looking at the particular case of older nurses (Watson et al, 2003). Management has a large measure of discretion over early retirement and whether individuals can work beyond the normal retirement age; however, they perceive themselves as being constrained by the rules of pension schemes and the accretion of custom and practice over the years. Generally managerial decisions seem to be tactical rather than guided by any overall policy towards older workers. From the employee's point of view the effect is that individual choice is exercised within the confines of organisational policy and the application of that policy can sometimes appear to be arbitrary and at other times very clearly targeted to the individual.

Although the employing organisation largely has the power to decide if and when individuals retire, this is generally used in an unsystematic way, so that it is not possible to conceptualise it as part of organisationally constructed retirement strategies. In so far as they exist they endure for relatively short periods or take varied forms in different parts of the organisation. For the individual employee the perception is of some choice, but highly unpredictable and often arbitrarily constrained choice. The effect of organisational policies is to create a myriad of different individual experiences and outcomes: this might be characterised as the organisation directing a stage play in which the actors occasionally chose their own lines. It is a stage on which individuals attempt to create their own plan of retirement but with varying success. Our cases would suggest that at least in the organisations studied here there is a diminishing expectation of the employer or pension scheme offering early retirement with enhanced pension. As to whether there is a more general change in expectations about early retirement on the part of employees, our evidence is more equivocal. People expected to be able to request early retirement if they wanted it, although many men and women assumed that they would work until state pension age.

There is a literature on how the structure of different occupational pension schemes may produce different incentives towards early retirement (see, for example, Blundell et al, 2002, and on the specific case of nurses see Watson et al, 2003, pp 18-19). This is significant in the context of companies shifting from defined benefit (final salary) to defined contribution (money purchase) schemes (see Vickerstaff et al, 2003, pp 73-4). The accepted wisdom is that final salary schemes may encourage people to seek early retirement at the peak of their career earnings or once they have clocked up the requisite number of pensionable years. Defined contribution (or money purchase) occupational pension schemes, which do not guarantee a given pension level but depend on the value of the pension pot at retirement, by contrast may encourage people to carry on working and increasing their pension savings if savings are only growing slowly (Disney and Hawkes, 2003, pp 62-3). Although this logic is persuasive our analysis suggests that you also need to factor in the willingness of the organisation to agree to an early retirement. Individuals may request early retirement but can be denied. The dynamics of pension scheme incentives are also conditioned by the prevailing patterns of management of older workers. If an organisation puts a premium on refreshing its workforce (for new skills, stamina, image or whatever reason) then requests for early retirement may be routinely accepted and the pension incentives may work in a relatively straightforward way. If the organisation seeks to retain its older worker force (because of recruitment difficulties, skills investment or a premium on experience) then pension incentives may be frustrated by organisational policy. The main outcome of a shift from defined benefit (final salary) to defined contribution (money purchase) schemes is that the burden of financial risk is shifted from the employer to employee.

3

Understanding pensions and retirement policies

Our research confirms the work of others that people find it difficult to understand their pensions and plan for retirement (see, for example, Anderson et al, 2000; Mayhew, 2001; Arthur, 2003). This is perhaps the more surprising because the vast majority of our respondents were in the comparatively lucky position of having an occupational pension, access to a company pension department and regular information on their pension status. Our research suggests three key things about this poor understanding and knowledge of pensions.

- People delay getting information about their options.
- People are confused about how pensions are calculated.
- People may be poorly advised.

We will discuss these in turn.

Need-to-know basis

A very common view among our respondents was that the information they had was on a need-to-know basis – that is, many of the employees had not got around to finding or working it all out as yet. Nevertheless, the majority of respondents across all three organisations were generally, with the odd exception, confident that organisations, if asked, gave useful information and pensions managers/ departments were helpful and approachable. However, this tendency to delay getting information meant that by not understanding their current situation many may fail to do things at the right time, for example in regard to additional voluntary contributions (AVCs). Higher paid and better educated respondents were more likely to have a clearer understanding of their current pension status but this group were not immune to the widespread ignorance and confusion:

"Would you be able to tell me a little about your pension and how it works?"

"No idea. I know it just – all I see on my payslip every month is 50-odd pound or whatever – Superann gone. Yes, it's attached to your earnings, the more you earn the more goes, and I just hope that when the time comes that it works. Yes. Figures are not my big thing. I put my financial things in the hands of other people and hope they know what they're doing quite honestly. Some do and some don't." (R21, female employed manager, LOCALGOV)

"What are your overall thoughts on the pension scheme?"

"Well it's a necessary evil isn't it?" (R61, male manual worker retired, TRANSPORT)

"I've got a rough idea of what the annual amount will be plus I've also got the option of taking a cash lump sum. I think if I take the cash lump sum I think it affects the overall figure but I'm not quite too sure by how much at the moment because I haven't actually been to somebody and said well if I take this how much will it affect this but.... Yes. I mean the more you earn ... the more you get on your basic money then the more you're going to get on your pension. But whether they take the last three years into consideration I'm not too sure." (R150, male white-collar employee, HEALTH PRODUCTS)

This suggests that it may not be enough to provide good information about pensions on demand; people may not demand it until too late. Even when our respondents received annual pension statements and forecasts they were often vague about the implications of their content:

"They do write to you once a year with an outline of what your pension could be if you retired at a certain age at a certain figure of remuneration. So it's well explained and it will give you sort of permutations of this. So it is very helpful that if you were thinking seriously of retiring in the next five years for example. So I think by next year, 2003, I'll look quite seriously at that document in January and begin to look at my future then I suppose. But I can't really remember what the heck is in there." (R51, male employed manager, LOCALGOV)

"I'm in the [TRANSPORT] pension fund. I joined it when I started here. They ask you if you want to join, and I thought why not. I don't really know how it works. They take it out of pay packet every month, and they put some in as well. And, I get a statement every year telling me what it's worth.

"I haven't looked into it much yet as I've got a few years to go yet.

"When I get nearer to retiring I'll have to find out more. But it's not something that's a priority for me now." (R104, male employed manual worker, TRANSPORT)

This may suggest that information is not being provided in a way that seems immediately significant to the individual or that people are not in a position to make anything of the information they receive. The need is not simply for more of it but for a greater understanding of the significance of the information available. This suggests that the real problem is the need for greater and better financial education and awareness.

Confusion about pension composition

Confusion about the mechanics of pensions was rife among all three cohorts of respondent: retired, pre-retired and employed. How pensions were calculated, who contributed what, trade offs between lump sums/monthly pensions and implications of working part-time or retiring early were a mystery to many people. This severely affects people's ability to think, or make decisions, about when to retire or the implications of downshifting.

"Well I understand that if I make it to 60, that there'll be a lump sum, and then you will get a small amount, a quarter of your salary every month, no sorry every year, not every month, every year – so that you've got a little bit of money coming in to go with your state pension." (R6, female employed supervisor, LOCALGOV)

"Yes that's right. It was some sort of ... I can't remember exactly. There is an equation the way the pension fund work out how much you get when you retire. It's something like one third of your wages plus this, plus that and it's tacked on to it. There is an equation. I can't remember exactly what it is." (R61, male manual worker retired, TRANSPORT)

"And that's something that's has really stopped me thinking too seriously about going part-time because I just assume that all these years that I've been working full-time would possibly count for very little then. I haven't gone into it but that's just my own understanding. I've probably read their booklet which I've got somewhere but off the top of my head I suppose like all pension schemes the employee pays x amount and the employer pays x amount and at the end of the time you get your pro rata payout on what a full-term pension would be.... Annually they do send a statement of the pension fund and scheme and how it's working and what it all is but it's all in small print and I never read it. I only look to see how much I'm getting." (R49, male white-collar worker retired, LOCALGOV)

If we couple this lack of understanding with the fact that some people will not have direct control over when they retire the impact is multiplied and, as Arthur concluded, those who have little choice about leaving work early may be in a very vulnerable position financially (2003, p 44). Another critical test of level of understanding is the point at which the individual has to manage the financial transition from paid work to retirement. For many people in occupational pension schemes a decision has to be made about how much to take as a lump sum or how much to have as a regular pension. Arthur, in her research on the financial circumstances of early retirement, highlighted this moment as a very significant one: "having a lump sum was a trigger for people to think about their financial future, and often seek financial advice" (2003, p 28). However, this could be rather late to confront these issues and a better understanding of pension composition and options earlier on would facilitate more considered planning and decisions. Appropriate information and understanding is of course dependent on being able to access reliable advice and knowing when you need it.

Lack of, or poor, advice

Another thread running through the accounts of our respondents was the lack of good advice at the right time, or the effects of earlier poor advice. Those with broken work histories and/or those who moved jobs or organisations particularly felt the risk of poor or absent advice. This was most likely to affect women and employees in industries with unstable employment patterns. In particular problems were likely to arise when decisions about transferring or keeping existing pensions had to be made.

"I believe I always thought I'd retire at 65. That was why I was stupid enough to ask to take my superannuation out when I left jobs. So I haven't got many years service. That's why I know I'll work until I'm 65 if I can." (R27, female employed social worker, LOCALGOV)

"So I paid into the National pension from 1973-1982 and then that was frozen then once I left the industry there. I then, as I say, joined the Coastguard ... which was

then the Principal Civil Servants Pension Scheme because you are a civil servant in the coastguard. And then because of the state of the [industry] then I decided to transfer ... into the Principal Civil Service one so that all transferred across. And then when I went back to [the industry] again I then rejoined the National Scheme, but that was as a new member then.... So I had to start again as a new member in 1990. And then I wasn't sure what to do with the Civil Service one so actually I was advised and I've obviously since found out that it was the wrong advice, I transferred that into a personal pension thing which eventually ended up in the Equitable Life and...." (R102, male employed manager, TRANSPORT)

"I had a deferred pension with British Gas and ... a few years ago I made enquiries about is it worthwhile transferring it to [HEALTH PRODUCTS]'s and the information I got then wasn't very good. It wasn't very helpful and the intermediary pensions people who [HEALTH PRODUCTS] brought in ... I wasn't very satisfied with what ... I couldn't decide from the information they gave me what to do so I left it there. But in the end I decided ... they involved another company about a year ago and the information they provided me with was a lot better about pensions and transferring my deferred pension and also I noticed that British Gas has changed some of their scheme details where I could get the deferred pension past 60. So then I thought well if I want to retire before then then the advantage to transfer it to [HEALTH PRODUCTS] where I could then have that before 60. So all in all that made me decide to transfer it and so I transferred it about a year ago." (R142, male employed manager, HEALTH PRODUCTS)

"The trouble is you don't find out [about whether to move pensions from one company to another] until you've done something that you've done it wrong. That's the trouble isn't it, and people are frightened because it's not explained to you. They don't tell you that." (R108, male employee manual worker, TRANSPORT)

There is an growing literature on the gender dimension of pensions and in particular the greater likelihood that women will have weak pension provision because of broken work histories and/or poor advice about the need to have a pension independent of their husbands. There were a number of women in the study who had paid a reduced National Insurance contribution or who had been unable to pay into the occupational pension initially because of working part-time. There were other cases where the woman's financial situation had worsened following a change in domestic circumstances:

"... nothing, nothing to fall back onto. And when my marriage ended in a divorce here again I had only worked part-time up to that point and I was not in a pension scheme. So my pension scheme only started I would say towards the end of 1987 so in total I've only got 14 years so I cannot afford to, even if I wanted to, or even go part-time I cannot do it because my pension is so small and if I retire, if I take retirement at the age of 60 apparently I will get a pension on a sliding scale. I don't know how it really quite works out but obviously I won't get 100%, I might get 25% less. That's my understanding. So there is no way I could take that drop so I have to work up until the age of 63 to draw some reasonable amount of pension." (R39, female white-collar employee, LOCALGOV)

This research confirms the conclusions of Arthur (2003, p 45) and others (for example, Evason and Spence, 2003) that information and advice may need to be targeted in different ways to different groups, particularly on women who are less likely to have built up pension entitlements over a long time.

Many retired and near-retired respondents in each of the organisations commented that it would be useful to have information or advice earlier. This was to some extent recognition of their own tendency to delay getting information.

"I'm quite happy receiving once a year a statement as to my particular position. I wouldn't say there was a big push by this particular company to do anything more than that. In fact that's probably one of the areas where I think they could do better.

To me, and I'm only talking from my experience [HEALTH PRODUCTS], they leave it far too late, much too late. I've had no discussion with anybody. Now they may take the view well it's not up to us to chase you mate. If you want to know about pensions you know where we are, come and talk to us. My view on it is that we should be more proactive. But when you get to the age of 20, or even when you first join the company, there should be a pension type intro to actually encourage people to pay more and think about their future. I know when you're young you haven't got a lot of money, you've got mortgages and marriages and Christ knows what. But at the same time you don't have to spend a lot of money. It seems to me like there's a catch up just before you're retiring, oh shit I should have chucked some money in the bloody pension fund." (R161, male managerial employee, HEALTH PRODUCTS)

"I think the courses they send you on are too late. I mean the course actually is brilliant. I went down to the hotel down at [A], somewhere around there, for three days and it was a seminar on retirement. How to benefit from your pensions and the additional voluntary contributions and all that. I had about three years after that before I retired and should be earlier than that." (R69, male manual worker retired, TRANSPORT)

However, it was also recognised that people did not find pension issues particularly interesting and perhaps companies could not reasonably be blamed for that:

"I mean the information is there whenever I've asked for it. As I say I believe the scheme is well run. How well it's publicised for all and sundry again I can't really comment because whenever I've needed or wanted to check on things the information has been there. So I can't really think of anything. I mean nobody really wants to think about their pensions when they're in their thirties....

"So I think however much they did they wouldn't get people to be terribly interested." (R146, male managerial employee, HEALTH PRODUCTS)

There was also always the possibility that information would be wrongly interpreted:

"If you offer too much information people can read too much into it and say I'm only 48, why is somebody offering me that information?" (R152, female employed manager, HEALTH PRODUCTS)

Summary

Most people do not find pensions interesting and even within 10 years of likely retirement many will not be thinking much about their possible circumstances in retirement. This supports Arthur's conclusion that "people often leave saving and planning until late in their lives" (2003, p 43). To some extent being in an occupational pension scheme may reassure people that it is not something they need or can do much about. Nevertheless, many of our interviewees were aware of the current changes to company pension schemes and some were experiencing a fall in the value of their personal savings as a result of the dull stock market. All three organisations in the study provided good information on individual pension status on demand and also regularly in the form of annual statements. HEALTH PRODUCTS was a leader in this respect issuing total benefit statements to employees – a measure heralded as best practice in recent government white papers (DWP, 2002, p 71; DWP, 2004, p 22). Yet, many people either paid scant attention to this information or were delaying getting details until some unspecified moment in the future. As a result they were poorly equipped to engage in retirement planning.

The provision of information and the availability of advice are clearly not sufficient to enable many people to plan the financial aspects of retirement. Information alone has little relevance unless it is placed in the context of a broader understanding of the core logic and financial principles of pensions. Most people do not have this understanding and cannot therefore effectively process or evaluate the information they are given. It may appear almost meaningless to them, so adding to the perceptions of risk and luck, rather than control,

in negotiating one's retirement with an employer. We can only conclude that the mere provision of good or even regular information cannot be presumed to equal education or empowerment.

This picture raises significant problems for public policy attempts to encourage individuals to think and plan more clearly for their retirements. Moves to "empower individuals to make their own decisions about retirement and the level of income they want in retirement" (DWP, 2004, p 3) need to appreciate that the employer often has discretion over when retirement will occur and that individuals may resist planning ahead. Good information available on demand is insufficient for the many who regard pensions as a distressed purchase. One respondent made a telling comment about the state pension:

"I don't know if you've had experience of this but do you find information is easy to access on the state pension?"

"No, it's not easy. It's not as readily available as the information that I receive from my employer and you begin to think that if every year there was some sort of statement or audit or idea of where you stand personally in terms of your state pension. I mean I've never understood any of it. I've never tried to understand it because I think I would be going around in circles. But if it was made clearer and simpler I think idiots would perhaps pay more attention to it really because it just seems as if it's a great big sort of ... you know how you went into a classroom and you see all these mathematical equations on a blackboard and you just look at that and think I don't understand any of it. No one ever paves the way to enter into that debate because you have nothing, no knowledge, no experiences of these ways of working and you're flummoxed by all these numbers so you just kind of give up on it. And it's pretty poor in a way that the country ... I think a lot of people probably feel like that in the country, except those that are working in economics and mathematics and any other business and finance. But there are people who don't work in those realms and have a very poor understanding of what they're doing with the state pension." (R51, male managerial employee, LOCALGOV)

There needs to be an emphasis on educating people about pensions and the importance of financial planning much earlier in their working careers. There is arguably a role for the education system, as acknowledged in a recent government paper (DWP, 2004, pp 19-20).

4

Choice

Phillipson (1982, 1999) reminds us that retirement is a relatively new phenomenon, largely a creation of the 20th century and institutionalised in the post Second World War period. For little more than 50 years have most people had any secure expectation of ending their working lives at a given age and obtaining a minimum level of financial security through a state pension. Subsequently, the trend towards early retirement (in particular for men) has destabilised the traditional life course notion of a 'set' retirement age of 60 or 65, with the result that the concept of 'retirement' itself has become more unpredictable and difficult to define. The fact that fewer people retire at the statutory retirement age means that the prospect of, planning for and experience of retirement are becoming more individualised. Routes into retirement and older age and their timing have also become more complex and varied.

Among our already-retired respondents the actual age of retirement had varied from 56 to 70, while among those still-employed expectations about age at retirement ranged from 55 to 65. Roughly half of the employees who were some distance away from retirement expected to retire at the normal retirement age for their organisation. Under half of those employees who were closer to retirement expected to retire at the normal retirement age. Only 12 employees in total expected to retire before they were 60. Whatever the individual's preferred age at retirement there was, however, the generally held view that this should be a matter of personal choice.

Normal retirement ages appeared to be very significant in structuring the way people thought about retirement age:

"... all things being equal I've got between now and 65 to decide, so no immediate plans." (R19, male white-collar employee, LOCALGOV)

"I think I've always just aimed for the 61 mark which was the industry retirement age anyway sort of thing so I've basically aimed for the 61." (R102, male employed manager, TRANSPORT)

"Well [TRANSPORT] will retire me on my pension at 60 so I've got just over six years to go." (R113, male employed manual worker, TRANSPORT)

"I left school at the age of 14 and will retire at 65. So that's not bad is it?" (R144, male manual employee, HEALTH PRODUCTS)

Normal retirement ages for the particular job acted as a benchmark for thinking about individual plans in conjunction with considerations about the point at which pension entitlements would kick in:

"Well because being a civil servant I knew I'd get my civil service pension and my state pension both when I was 60 so I've always known I wouldn't work beyond age 60. So I'll work until 60, unless I win the lottery, but as soon as I'm 60 then I shall stop." (R10, female white-collar employee, LOCALGOV)

For those on lower incomes and with weaker pension entitlements the state pension age was equally an important target for planning.

"So, would the state pension influence your decision as to when to retire?"

"Not significantly. It might make a difference as to whether you stopped two or three years short of state pension or seven or eight. A couple of years probably won't make a lot of difference, but 10 or 12 years short of it, it might." (R18, male white-collar employee, LOCALGOV)

Research on early retirement decisions suggests individual variables such as financial worth, health status and opportunities for different activities in retirement are significant factors in structuring the choices that individuals make and their degree of satisfaction in retirement (McGoldrick and Cooper, 1994; Maule et al, 1996). These analyses tend to focus on the individual and the social but ignore the key intermediate and mediating variable of the organisation from which most retire. As we saw in an earlier section, management within the employing organisation has a large amount of discretion about early retirement but it is typical for organisations to have a normal retirement age at which people are expected to stop work. Individual factors interact with the dynamics of

organisational policies to produce various possible retirement scenarios. It is better to conceptualise these as scenarios rather than trajectories as individual and organisational circumstances may change so that the individual's aspirations or expectations alter or have to be modified. The idea of a scenario is useful also because a factor, which in one individual case may predispose to early retirement, may in another case be a factor for staying at work. As individuals enter the 'retirement zone' they meet a complex mixture of factors that condition outcomes. All the different individual and organisational variables are present in a particular individual's retirement scenario but the pattern of interactions is different from case to case.

In Figure 2 we set out the key individual factors that interact with the patterns of management discretion within the retirement zone (see Figure 1, p 9). From the study it is possible to identify four broad categories of retirement scenario which in turn are subdivided according to the individual or organisational factors that are key in placing an individual into that scenario (see retirement scenarios box, p 20). These four stylised descriptions are not to be seen as distinct

Figure 2: Individual factors that interact with management discretion

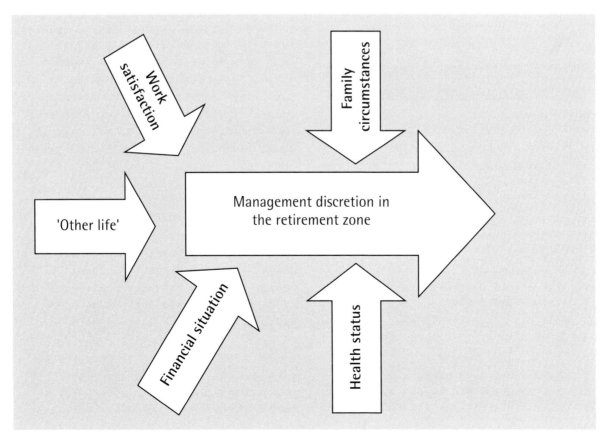

categories; an individual may move between scenarios as their personal situation or organisational circumstances change. Rather, they provide a means of analysing a number of key influences on the retirement pathways of individuals. We will discuss each scenario in turn.

Happy and keen to retire

A majority of our employed respondents looked forward to retiring and had plans and ideas as to what they hope to do. The retired as a group exhibited more mixed reactions. There were both positive and negative reasons for being keen to retire. Some people were focused on what came next whereas others were clearer about what they wanted to leave behind.

Financial situation

Individuals' financial situations obviously provide a significant backdrop for aspirations and plans about retirement. This research confirms earlier work that a distinction must be made between those who retire in relative economic security and health and those who face more uncertain futures: what have been referred to as the 'two nations in retirement'. For those in well-paid and stable occupations there will have been scope to secure the retirement future.

Retirement scenarios

1. Happy and keen to retire:
   - financial situation
   - looking forward to other things
   - done enough.

2. Forced, or felt forced, to retire:
   - age
   - early retirement.

3. Do not want to retire:
   - enjoy work
   - afraid of retirement.

4. Blown off course:
   - family circumstances
   - individual health status
   - organisational policies.

"I've been for quite a few years paying in my AVCs to the limit that I could pay in a year with the view to be financially able to retire at 57 which would be a year and a half from now. But that's not to say that that's when I will necessarily want to go. What I wanted to do was set things up so that financially I've got that option." (R148, male managerial employee, HEALTH PRODUCTS)

"No. I retired early. Normal retirement age is 65. [TRANSPORT]'s retirement age ... was 62. I actually retired just before I was 61. Do you want to know the reason why I retired?"

"Yes please."

"Because I could. It's as simple as that. With the pension. With what savings and investments I've already got. It gave me a nudge because physically I was becoming a bit of a wreck and I have a lot of problems with my neck, this, that and the other and I thought retirement seemed to be a good thing. And I could afford to so I did it." (R65, male manager retired, TRANSPORT)

"I paid a lot of AVCs into my pension fund over the years to boost it up.... But that was the main factor. I think I thought by the time I get to 60 I'd have had 33 years of shift work and it's time to give shift work a kick and I've got the money to be able to afford to do it, to retire so that was the decision really. I just couldn't see the point in working after I was 60." (R122, male manual employee retired, HEALTH PRODUCTS)

Here the financial incentives offered by the final salary schemes are working to condition individuals' choices. However, the ability to retire early as they planned is still conditioned by their employer's willingness to accede to their request. Of course, for many, financial planning will be a household matter and may involve strategies around two incomes or pensions:

"I don't want to retire without him. It's not that I can't fill my day but we're a very close couple and we do everything together and we wanted to go together. He obviously at 52, which he is now, he was looking at going at 55 but we've been monitoring our pension very carefully with the pension department and he will have maximum pension by about March 2004 so the decision to go is based on his full pension. I have about ... I'll have about 90% full pension which linked to him we feel is enough and we were financially able to make the decision to go." (R152, female managerial employee, HEALTH PRODUCTS)

Thus, for some the decision to retire early is rooted in the fact that it has been possible to make financial plans and see them bear fruit. For others, finances are precisely the reason why retirement will be delayed:

"It's my financial situation which will really compel me to work until the age of 63. Otherwise I would ideally be quite happy and would like to retire at 60 and perhaps over the next few years work four days a week and just have a day to myself because I would like to develop other things which I would like to pursue when I retire.... I have to have enough money to live on when I retire because I've got a mortgage and that mortgage I don't finish paying off until I'm 63 so I'm totally trapped." (R39, female white-collar employee, LOCALGOV)

"So when you come to retire what do you think will be the most important factor to influence your decision as to when to stop working?"

"Well I suppose in all fairness it would have to be finance. You know if I could afford to retire I think it obviously makes retirement that much easier. If you can carry on living to the standard that you're used to.... If all of a sudden you find out, well hold on a minute I can't do this and I can't do that and I can't afford to go there and I've got to get rid of my car, then it's going to put a sour taste in your mouth about retirement." (R105, male manual employee, TRANSPORT)

Looking forward to other things

Retirement was eagerly awaited by many as providing opportunities to pursue their 'other life': to do all the things they had not had time,

or not enough time, to do while working. For some this might entail quite grandiose plans about living abroad, while for others it was more routine activities, but what they all shared was enjoying having discretion over their own time.

"And would you say you looked forward to your retirement?"

"Oh you bet your life. Yes. That's why I didn't do a day over."

"OK. Is there anything in particular you looked forward to about it or ...?"

"Yes. All my life I've never had enough time. I've always had to go to work and I'm tickled pink about it now that I can just get up and do exactly what I want. So time to myself was the main answer....

"No. It's absolutely true what they say, you don't know how you managed to go to work." (R75, male manual retired, TRANSPORT)

"And are you looking forward to your retirement?"

"Very much, yes."

"Do you have any idea what you think your main activity will be when you're retired?"

"Well, probably going down to France and looking after – we have a place down in France – going down and looking after the place in France, and generally doing all the things that you like to do in the warmth. So it would be quite nice." (R6, female employed manager, LOCALGOV)

"Is there anything in particular that you're looking forward to?"

"Basically doing what I want to when I want to do it.... I mean I play golf and I do quite a lot of further education. At the moment I'm doing a Microsoft course which eventually will be a Microsoft Certified Engineer so sort of things like that would give me more time to study on them than being pre-occupied with other things.... Like I said I'll probably move somewhere that's a lot cheaper to live. A lot of people move to Spain and places like that because it's a more healthy environment." (R111, male managerial employee, TRANSPORT)

Here the pull of interests, hobbies and activities is significant in the retirement process; people are looking forward to having discretion over how they spend their time.

Done enough

Many of the respondents displayed a strong work ethic, evidenced by pride at having worked for many years or, among the men, by having unbroken employment histories. A corollary of this for some was a profound feeling that just as one had a duty to work one also deserved to retire at a reasonable point:

"Is there anything in particular that you're looking forward to about it?"

"It's quite pathetic but it's not having to get up every morning from Monday to Friday at the same time. If I want to stay in bed another hour or whatever I can do it and I can do what I want. I mean I've been working 40 years now and I just feel it's enough." (R60, female manual employee, LOCALGOV)

"The only thing is early retirement. I'd like to see that come back. You know, I think 40 years of shift work is enough for any human being and I think that should be recognised." (R109, male managerial employee, TRANSPORT)

"Well I mean I think I've worked all my life.... I mean I'm entitled to a bit of life. All I've done is from school to work. I wouldn't have had a life. Do you know what I mean?" (R153, male manual employee, HEALTH PRODUCTS)

Such a view is institutionalised in the 85-year rule in local government, whereby if your age and years of service add up to 85 you are entitled to retire on a full pension. The fact that the ability to go under the 85-year rule was at management's discretion in LOCALGOV rankled some respondents who perceived it to be unjust:

"And I've actually worked with somebody up there at the moment and he has worked man and boy and I think he's 54. He's near enough done the 85. I think in two years time he done it. Can I go then? No you can't because they're not going to let you retire. But I've done the 85-year rule. It's management discretion. So we do get a lot of those. I mean they're coming up and saying well why can't I go? And we've got to say LOCALGOV says no." (Trade union representative, LOCALGOV)

Forced, or felt forced, to retire

A significant minority of our respondents from across all three organisations felt that they had had little choice about when to retire. Normal retirement ages were the main culprit whereas others felt they had been forced to accept or go for early retirement.

Age

Fixed retirement ages are likely to come under increasing scrutiny as we approach the enactment of age discrimination legislation in 2006. In general, among our respondents, even for those who felt personally unaffected by the presence of an organisation's normal retirement age (NRA), there was agreement that people should be allowed to continue working beyond the NRA if they wished to and were fit to do so. Fixed retirement ages were experienced as arbitrary and unfair:

"Well really the fact that I had to go at 65. I would go along with this idea that you should be able to work as long as you feel that you are able to do the job.... I wasn't pleased to retire mentally." (R46, female white-collar retired, LOCALGOV)

"Well that really wasn't a decision on my part at all. It's [TRANSPORT]'s policy to retire you at 61 and in actual fact I would have liked to have stayed because I was on a good wage and I would have liked to have stayed on perhaps another two or three years although I was getting a bit worn out and stressed and everything but I would have liked to have had that full pay for a little bit longer before I retired but I had no choice." (R61, male manager retired, TRANSPORT)

"Well to be honest with you whatever they had offered me if I had the chance I would have worked until I was 65." (R62, male manual employer, had to retire at 63, TRANSPORT)

"Well I've got no decision to me. I've got to go so.... Because I'm 65. Which is the latest age that you'd have to retire here." (R153, male manual employee, HEALTH PRODUCTS)

On the basis of this research we can suggest that any proposals to remove normal retirement ages will find favour among employees and especially among lower paid workers, who, as in the case of TRANSPORT, now find that they have to retire some years before they are entitled to the state pension.

'Voluntary' early retirement

The 'decision' to retire early may still be a more or less forced one for many people, for example those who take 'voluntary' early retirement under pressure from their employer or due to ill-health, or those who are made redundant in their fifties or sixties. In the waves of company and organisation downsizing that occurred in the 1980s and 1990s, research has documented that many people who were offered an early retirement package or voluntary redundancy felt pushed or forced to take it when in fact they would have preferred to carry on working. It is in this constrained context that individual biography and health, finance, domestic circumstances and confidence may play their roles. However, among our respondents there were relatively few that had felt forced to retire in this sense:

"So moving on to your retirement decision now. At what stage in your career would you say you seriously started to think about retirement?"

"Well I tend to be a bit of a workaholic and I never ever gave it any thought whatsoever.... No. I retired when I was 57, solely because the [unit] closed.... I got like a severance pay, an early retirement

package, part of it was I think £30,000 which was tax free which was gave to me." (R139, male manual retired, HEALTH PRODUCTS)

The relatively small numbers in this category among our respondents may reflect the general trend among organisations to reduce the number of early retirement packages offered. This suggests that the numbers of involuntary early retired may be declining. Nevertheless, there were more interviewees who felt they had no option but to ask for early retirement because they were disgruntled with what was going on at work:

"And then all of a sudden I found that I was doing jobs that I was doing 20 years ago, helping out where with a job I'd done 20 years ago so I just turned around and saw my boss and I said to him what's going on? I'm not looking to retire for another two years. What's going on? And this was the original manager. He couldn't really.... He said oh I didn't understand. I didn't realise that was going on. But it didn't really change. Nothing really changed. So in the end I went in and asked him to make me redundant. He couldn't do that so I applied for early retirement and got that." (R137, male white-collar retired, HEALTH PRODUCTS)

"OK. And would you say you're looking forward to retirement at all?"

"Extremely."

"Is that for any particular reason or...?"

"Yes. My reason is I think HEALTH PRODUCTS, well, my department, are treating me like ... well the only thing I can put it down as is a leper. Don't get me wrong. There are people on this site that I know and work with that can't understand why I've been kicked to one side. I mean basically I'm coming in and it's just passing the time of day. I mean that's why I forgot about you, I was sitting on the computer playing around." (R144, male manual employee, HEALTH PRODUCTS)

The dominant outcome for employers offering enhanced early retirement packages in this study was to create a constituency of employees hoping for the offer of a package but who recognised that their chances of getting one were slight! In all three organisations there was a history of periods in the past when significant numbers of people had left early with enhanced pensions. These examples were very much part of organisational memory:

"I know early retirement is a very expensive option. I suppose I do have some views. My husband and I had a very nice holiday last year. We'd been married 25 years and we had an around the world trip and we went on a cruise as part of that and there were two people on there, both in their early sixties, looked in really good shape and they were sort of saying how they'd both been able to retire early from the Ministry of Defence. I think they were probably about 55 and on fairly good salaries and they appreciated that they were probably the last of that generation, the last generation, that was able to do that. So I suppose I'm a bit resentful that that isn't likely to be an option for me or other people of my generation because there were some very handsome packages being paid out five and longer years ago which the local authority are still having to ... and other government bodies are still having to pay for and they're not going to ... unlikely they will recur." (R53, female managerial employee, LOCALGOV)

In the case of some senior staff in TRANSPORT there had been an early retirement scheme in the national pension arrangements allowing people to go at 57 without a reduction in pension. This option was removed in 1999 and among the interviewees there were people who had been able to go at 57 and others who had missed it by being just too young. The effect of this sort of change in policy (referred to as a 'guillotine' by one interviewee) was often a deep sense of unfairness, that for no cause of one's own the benefits a colleague had received were not available to you.

Those who do not want to retire

The third important subgroup of our sample were those who did not think, or claimed not to think, about retirement at all. They did not want

to retire and hence had avoided contemplating it. This could be for positive or negative reasons. There were those who loved their work, wanted to carry on doing it or who assumed that they would always be active in some work capacity. These people were very distinct from those who were not particularly attached to their current work but who feared retirement and hence viewed it in a very negative light.

Enjoying work

Some people simply enjoy their work and want to carry on doing it:

"I never, never thought about retirement.... When I don't feel happy, that will be the day. But all along ... there are lots of reasons why I want to still stay on at work and I've said one is because I still feel I've got something to contribute. I still feel active enough. And my health at the moment, touch wood, is OK. I don't feel it a burden to go to work. You've got your colleagues, which you have a laugh and a joke with them. You also feel that if they've got burdens they call me mum. So you sort of feel that you're doing something or you cheer them up if they feel down. Lots of things really." (R90, female white-collar employee, TRANSPORT)

"So overall would you say you're looking forward to retirement or not?"

"No, not really. I mean I'm looking forward to not having to work as much as I do but I think if you look forward to retirement it's like wishing your life away. And that sort of worries me when people are sort of counting the days until they retire. I think crikey how depressing." (R40, female white-collar employee, LOCALGOV)

"So did you look forward to retiring?"

"Well no not really. I suppose in a nutshell I was a workaholic really. I always enjoyed what I was doing and in latter years I've had jobs where I was my own boss anyway which makes life a lot easier doesn't it?" (R24, male manual retired, LOCALGOV)

Others had carried on working beyond normal retirement age or hoped to do so:

"I'm one of those people who likes a structure to life.... I mean even when I'm considering retiring I just never think I will be sitting at home. I've already chosen two charities I would like to work for. I'm not one of these people who can just stay at home. Do you know?" (R39, female white-collar employee, LOCALGOV)

"So I worked until I was 67 in actual fact. But I enjoyed it. I really enjoyed it. The only person who didn't enjoy it was the wife because she was looking forward to having me at home but now she has got me at home I think she wishes I was still working!" (R25, male manual retired, LOCALGOV)

If not actively rejected, retirement for some may be difficult to accommodate as a status consistent with the range of activities they are involved in and expect to do in the future:

"I have a secondary career. I'm a writer as well ... and I'd like to actually maybe start taking that on board full-time."

"What do you think will be your main activity when you're retired?"

"Yes, writing and performing.... I've got choice and that's what I need, yes. Choices and the opportunity to work on if I wanted to and the opportunity to give up before the end of my working life if I wanted to pursue another career." (R51, male managerial employee, LOCALGOV)

For those who enjoy their work the presence of a normal retirement age is seen as unnecessary and cruel.

Afraid of retirement

For others retirement was not something to look forward to but something to dread, a landscape without structure, purpose or the security of belonging:

"Yes. If you get up in the morning and you haven't got to go to work it would be quite a strange feeling I should think, unless you plan it. I mean some people say I've got plenty to do, I can't wait to retire because I've got loads to do but I don't know.... I'm fingers crossed hoping that within the next 10 years that things are going to change and I can stay here until I'm 65. That's my own belief....

"I think because I've always been an active person and just at the moment I can't see what I would do once I retire. I would probably ... I mean I've spoken about it at home and I would probably take a part-time job because I think that I keep myself fairly healthy and fit and I don't just want to sit at home and rot. I think I've got more in me than that." (R105, male manual employee, TRANSPORT)

"No. I'm not looking forward to retirement. I'd rather avoid it.... You still need to be engaged with people. I can't see myself.... You've got to keep on firing as long as you've got bullets and so retirement is something that I'd rather avoid if I could but if I have to do it then I'll obviously have to do it. And the state retirement benefits are not sustainable at my sort of lifestyle that one gets accustomed to. So I tend to push things like pensions and state retirement benefits into one ... into the shade, into a grey area where it's really not going to be sustainable and I'd rather have an income that I am in control of, rather than someone else being in control of." (R168, male managerial employee, HEALTH PRODUCTS)

"So would you say that you looked forward to your retirement or not really?"

"No I don't think I did. I would have preferred to work on.... I think it's having a bit of purpose really, a bit of purpose in something to do. There's a reason to get up, you have to go to work, you work, you earn money, you earn money and you can do whatever, so just one thing follows the other. You just need a reason to get out of bed in the morning, really, I think." (R79, male manual retired, TRANSPORT)

Men predominated in this category of respondents who could almost be said to fear retirement. The centrality of paid work to their lives and identities meant that retirement appeared as a formless threat. This group, who could be said to be almost in denial about the inevitability of future retirement, are probably most at risk of not seeking information or advice about pensions at an early enough point.

Blown off course

The last subgroup of our respondents were people who had made particular plans with regards to retirement or who had simply assumed that they would carry on to normal retirement age but who found themselves 'blown off course' by a change in circumstances. Much of the literature on retirement concentrates on individual variables such as health status or domestic circumstances as key factors impacting on an individual's retirement decisions and trajectory. Our research confirms the significance of these factors but adds two complications to the normal analyses. First, personal factors can have different impacts depending on the organisation the individual works for. For example, the effects of ill-health or caring responsibilities are refracted through organisational policies in the sense of what is made possible or impossible by organisational policy or practice. Second, the influence of particular health or domestic factors may dispose one person to retire while strengthening the resolve of another to continue working. It is overly simple to assume that the causal affect of poor health, one's own or that of dependants or family members, is in one direction only.

Family circumstances

Family circumstances were a consistently present factor in interviews with employees and the retired. For example, the presence of an ailing partner, although clearly impinging on someone's thinking about retirement, could generate quite opposite preferences:

"In my mind I've always determined that I would retire at 60 but it really would depend on what my circumstances were when I am 59. I'm not sure how long in advance that you have to say to them yes I want to go at this age or not but my husband is quite ill and so it would really depend on where we were in two years' time because I might not feel that I want to stay at home if I was on my own. But if he was, bless him, still around then that whole thing could influence the way that my mind would be working, if that makes sense." (R60, female manual employee, LOCALGOV)

"Are you looking forward to retirement?"

"Not really because my wife has not been too good with regards to her nerves at the moment and although she works I feel that I'm treading on egg shells when I go home and all that so I'd rather stick it out a bit for the moment. So not really seriously. I don't think I could stand it." (R165, male manual employee, HEALTH PRODUCTS)

For some people, women in particular, a change in domestic circumstances profoundly affected their financial status and hence their attitude towards retirement:

"Have you seriously started to think about retirement, would you say?"

"At the moment no. Because what's happened to me in the last two years, I've – my husband has left me, done adultery, and I'm getting – he's divorcing me, so it's not like I've got a partner and that I've been with 20-odd years, which I have been married to 25 years and you're building up for retirement. Now it's a new lease of life and I'm having to get my progression in my, and get promotion in my career, so I can earn more money and pay more into a pension and – but I'm living for today really. Although I have got a pension and I've got life assurance and other insurance, although I'm covered that way, I feel at the moment for my son I'm worth more dead than alive, you know! He wouldn't have me say that, but financially I am. I've got myself covered quite strongly, because I think it's important. I know one day, I'd like to retire before 65 if I can, but I don't know what's round the corner do I?" (R17, female white-collar employee, LOCALGOV)

"And when my marriage ended in a divorce here again I had only worked part-time up to that point and I was not in a pension scheme. So my pension scheme only started I would say towards the end of 1987 so in total I've only got 14 years so I cannot afford to, even if I wanted to, or even go part-time I cannot do it because my pension is so small.... I have to work up until the age of 63 to draw some reasonable amount of pension." (R39, female employee, LOCALGOV)

"I tended to hope that I'd retire at 55.... But I had problems. I was divorced and I was paying maintenance obviously on my children and my wife and I couldn't afford to put it into AVCs until I got to 50 when my last child left home and went to work. So it was then that I could start putting in AVCs. So then I thought well 60 and as I said to you earlier it just wasn't quite enough." (R127, male manual, retired at 62 from HEALTH PRODUCTS)

For others a change in domestic life made earlier retirement less attractive:

"I wanted to retire at 55, until I was widowed, and then I thought well I'd better carry on till I'm 60. Always when my husband was alive I kept saying 55 and I'll pack it in, because he didn't like me doing the nights." (R21, female employee, LOCALGOV)

Individual health status

It is widely acknowledged in the literature on older workers that health issues are a key factor in whether people continue working up to retirement age or not. This is especially so for less-skilled manual workers. In this research, too, health was found to be a factor in people's thinking about the prospect of retirement – that is, if they were to have a significant health problem in the future they expected this to have an impact on their retirement decision. However, for the already-retired, health had in reality been a much less prominent factor in their retirement process.

Where health had been a major factor it often combined with other circumstances. In the following case, individual health, spouse's health, financial situation and organisational change all coalesce to form the retirement scenario:

"... the UK commercial arm of HEALTH PRODUCTS were moving to [R] and that happened about 18 months ago. So I didn't want to move to [R]. I was too close to retirement to consider that. I took up a completely new post that had just been invented and I just got into that and my wife developed breast cancer and I suffered from depression. And it came to a stage where it was going back into quite a high tech, quite high pressured environment after I'd been depressed and I was still suffering from panic attacks or contemplating something else and retirement for me was the best option.

"Well I knew my pension was going to be adequate. I wanted to spend time with my wife who is just recovering from surgery." (R121, male manager retired, HEALTH PRODUCTS)

In other instances, reactions to a similar health problem can vary dramatically according to other surrounding circumstances:

"So all these things came together you see, the breast cancer, the office closing and me being 65 all happened within a few weeks of each other. So retirement was not an option, it was absolutely necessary." (R44, female white-collar retired, LOCALGOV)

"It all evolves a little bit around my health issue. I was diagnosed with breast cancer five years ago this coming July 9th and with the [HEALTH PRODUCTS] healthcare I actually, and it's not said lightly, owe them my life because they moved so quickly and within 10 days I was on full treatment which I would not have got under the NHS. The type of tumour I had grew to the size of an orange in a matter of four months so it was an extremely virulent and bad case and basically it cost [HEALTH PRODUCTS] ... the initial treatment cost [HEALTH PRODUCTS] £25,000 because all the bills came in. So what I very much wanted to do was be monitored under the private health cover. We hadn't made any decisions to retire but it was very linked around this cover that [HEALTH PRODUCTS] were giving us and I wanted to at least see how it went because there was a 20% chance of it coming back in the first

12 months and then it's about 10% and obviously there are no guarantees but it could come back tomorrow or the year after that. So a decision of whether or not to keep on the private health cover is a big decision for us so thinking about the cost." (R152, female managerial employee, HEALTH PRODUCTS)

We would suggest that where large-scale surveys clearly demonstrate links between health and the retirement decision, they may also obscure the mechanisms that connect them. While for a majority the consequences of ill-health may be predictable, for a significant minority, they may operate quite differently. There is also evidence to suggest that in a number of cases ill-health may retrospectively be seen as the cause or explanation for early retirement when it did not figure as the key reason for leaving work at the time (Beatty and Fothergill, 2003a, pp 147-9). The organisation also plays an important mediating role in how it responds, or fails to respond, to an individual's changing health status. A study of the work aspirations of older nurses found that relatively minor changes to work patterns or schedules could affect whether someone felt able to carry on working or not (Watson et al, 2003, pp 14-22).

Organisational policies

Changes in organisational policies, work practices or work location can all have the effect of altering someone's disposition towards the retirement issue. Those nearing retirement age may see such changes as just an extra push to get out early:

"That's right. I didn't want to retire actually. That might be a turn up for the books but no I was rather reluctant to retire. I'd come and I think I was getting to the stage where I was trying to keep up with the things and performance is everything in [HEALTH PRODUCTS] and I realised that it was getting near time to go. That was one of the reasons I decided I wouldn't ... I mean I could have gone on a bit longer, another year maybe." (R135, male manager retired, HEALTH PRODUCTS)

"So I found that I was slowly dropping behind on the new technology and because my old technology was there then they obviously didn't give me the new technological stuff so I found myself in a vacuum just doing routine work. You know oh he's a silly old sod, we'll give it to him.... So if you started to slip down not only did you start to lose pay but when you started to get your bonus at the end of it then that was down. So it became a situation for me that was becoming intolerable and so that was another reason that I felt the time had come to retire." (R127, male manual worker retired, HEALTH PRODUCTS)

In other scenarios organisational changes might impact with health issues to change the individual's outlook:

"Well I mean to be honest [TRANSPORT] retirement is 63 and I had planned to work until 63. That's what I planned and that's what I wanted to do.... I retired in September 2000 when I was 60. I would say I started to think about it in the June, simply because we came back from holiday in April time and this is when they put us into this Call Centre in this cramped position and I started to get all this trouble I had and of course come the June the doctor put me on a high dose of steroids which was doing the trick. I was feeling alright and of course as my steroids came down and the aches and pains continued I thought to myself I couldn't do another three years like this." (R72, female white-collar worker retired, TRANSPORT)

The impact of organisational changes will vary according to other individual factors; some may thrive on change, while others just feel they have had enough. Active consideration of the impact of organisational changes on older workers might in some cases reduce the likelihood of someone opting for early retirement. Relatively small changes to work routines or tasks, where possible, might extend the working life of particular individuals.

Summary

Respondents across the organisations and in all cohorts were generally agreed that the timing and manner of retirement should be a matter of personal judgement and choice: just as people should not be forced to retire at a given age, nor should they be forced to continue when they felt they were ready to go. This suggests that retirement is seen as a consumption good, a consumer choice or right, which people expect to have a measure of control over. In reality, we have seen how a combination of personal factors and organisational practices serve to produce both opportunities and threats to individual choice.

Among our interviewees, those farthest away from likely retirement tended to rate health as a key factor in exit decisions whereas, for those who had retired, own health and health of family members were less significant. Rather organisational factors, such as being able to draw a decent pension, were more important. Using the concept of retirement scenarios we have seen how contingent individual retirement decisions and trajectories are. The organisation provides the stage on which individual scenarios are played out: the application of early retirement rules, changes in work practices, discretion over normal retirement ages, whether to re-employ someone on a consultancy basis and so on. All the variables are present in the individual scenario (finance, health, domestic circumstances, the pull of the other life, work satisfaction) but the pattern of interactions differs from person to person, according to the structure of individual preferences and the specific pressures coming from the employing organisation.

5

Downshifting employment in the transition to retirement

Another major theme of the research was to investigate the extent of interest in, and potential barriers to, people downshifting their workload prior to full retirement. This could take a number of forms:

- bridge employment: that is, leaving the career employer and finding another job to bridge the gap until state retirement age;
- self-employment;
- downshifting workload with the existing employer by reducing hours worked;
- downshifting workload with the existing employer by taking on a different role often of less seniority or stress.

This research confirms other work, which demonstrates that many people who go through an early retirement process from one employer continue to seek, and find, paid employment in the labour market (Dench and Norton, 1996; Phillipson, 2002). However, it is clear that the ability to find another job is strongly correlated with levels of skills and qualifications and local labour market factors (Beatty and Fothergill, 2003b; Lissenburgh and Smeaton, 2003). Poorly qualified older workers in a depressed local labour market will find it difficult to find a bridge and are far more likely to end up dependent on benefits. It is therefore hypothesised that one potential response to the low labour force participation rates of older workers is to explore the possibilities for individuals to undertake bridge employment, or in other words downshift, with their existing employer. Another response to early withdrawal from the labour market is to consider the possibilities for flexible or gradual retirement in which individuals can reduce work commitment and draw some pension in the period prior to full retirement (Taylor, 2002, p 22; DWP, 2004, p 14). One aim of the research

reported here was to test ideas about, and the practical feasibility of, downsizing as part of a process towards full retirement. In this section we look at these issues from two perspectives: first, the experience of, or aspirations in relation to, bridge employment among our respondents and, second, organisational and individual responses to the idea of downshifting within the existing employment prior to retirement.

Bridge employment

In relation to bridge employment between retirement from the organisation and state pension age and full retirement there are a number of different themes that emerge from the study. It should be noted, however, that we do not look at self-employed routes to full retirement in this research. First, expected or actual level of income in retirement is a major source of differentiation; higher salaried employees who will have decent pensions may consider continuing work for the interest, or to pick up something new or different:

"So if I can I envisage a part-time job."

"Yes. Would that be in the same sort of area or something totally different?"

"Totally different."

"Have you got anything in mind?"

"Yes. I've played cricket for a number of years and I live very close to [X] Cricket Club and I've played for them for a number of years and they've got a vacancy for a groundsman coming up." (R149, male employed professional, HEALTH PRODUCTS)

"Well actually probably I'll have enough to do when I do [retire] because if I keep my NVQ assessing up to date there's no reason why when I retire I can't do that. So there is that option. I also do an awful lot of dressmaking and that and I might do it more professionally then as opposed to now." (R36, female employed manager, LOCALGOV)

Those in lower income groups are more likely to need to try to find employment to bridge the income gap before receiving the state pension. This was particularly an issue for interviewees who worked for TRANSPORT because of the normal retirement ages of 61, 62 and 63 for different groups of employees. Lower income individuals are likely to be able to find only even less well paid and/or casual work.

"So that was my decision all along that I'd go into security, which I did do, which I am doing still, I still am doing.... This is a different kind of job I'm doing now.... This is full-scale security I'm on now which I wasn't before.... I'm not retired. I'm still working full-time. In fact I'm working more hours now than what I did with TRANSPORT." (R68, male manual employee, retired from TRANSPORT)

"So is the HGV driving you do now, is that for the farmer or the farm...?"

"Well I do but I do a bit for an agency as well. In the bad weather now they haven't been able to get the potatoes out of the ground anyway so I do a bit for Skelmersdale which is night trunk. I take it up to Glasgow, drop the trailer off, pick another one up and come back again. I like the night. It's quiet. It's peaceful.... Well she wants me to give up working and I say oh ... I've always had plenty of money in my pocket and I always like to have money in my pocket and I think OK when I get to 65 OK I'll be able to live comfortably and all that but I always think to myself an extra couple of hundred quid would come in handy." (R69, male manual employee, retired from TRANSPORT)

In this study those working in the public sector seemed to have greater opportunities for finding work in the same sector or organisation than those in the private sector, but it would not be safe to generalise this finding. It was also the case that a significant group of respondents from LOCALGOV had worked beyond the normal retirement age often in part-time jobs such as caretakers, cleaners or lollipop duties – frequently taking up such jobs after careers in other departments or sectors:

"... it was granted, everything was very amicable, that was fine, and it was agreed I could go early retirement and I gave about four or five months' notice, you know it was fine – and that was it basically. And – but just during the period of notice I got another temporary job within [LOCALGOV] and apart from a week's break I've worked ever since only part-time.... Yes, I've always worked for [LOCALGOV] in various ways. I did a two years' post early retirement job in the Educational Welfare Service before I became a Governor Support Officer." (R19, male, originally retired from a personnel officer post in the LOCALGOV at the age of 50)

In general, managers and others with professional expertise are much more likely to benefit from the organisation's discretion in letting an individual continue work, or come back on a consultancy basis.

"Yes they've come back as consultants or on a consultancy basis."

"And is that in any particular part of the organisation?"

"No, just general. And I would hazard a guess it is probably part of this headcount business. A consultant doesn't show up as a head.... No. I think it's probably in certain areas. I mean gardeners for example, there's no way they would want a gardener back as a consultant." (R126, male manager retired, HEALTH PRODUCTS)

"The way they're talking at the moment I go part-time when I am 62 and I should be able to finish when I'm 64 and become a consultant." (R174, male employed manager, HEALTH PRODUCTS)

"Well we've got a typical example of the [B] on my vessel at the moment. He is coming up to 62. He wants to carry on but they say he can't carry on because of the terms and conditions so what he has to do is he has to terminate his service at 62 but he can actually come back after a break of a fortnight."

"Oh I see. So he would be back on a different contract of employment."

"He will be back on a different contract. That's right. So he wouldn't be on the same contract that he's on now. He would be on a different contract and it would probably mean less money." (R103, male employed manager, TRANSPORT)

However, this process is not without its critics and it is another area of management discretion, which is sometimes perceived as unfair:

"Yes we have people that leave on the Friday and come back on the Monday as consultants."

"How does that go down with colleagues?"

"It doesn't because it's totally unfair. They've had a big pay-off.

"They're getting their pension and they come in and they work it so that they know exactly how much they can earn before paying any tax because they're getting their pension as well and people just see it as unfair because they're generally doing special projects that are of interest and junior members of staff and women in particular think well why don't they let me do that? So there is resentment." (R9, male white-collar employee, LOCALGOV)

"If you're quite high up then some people come back as a consultant, but you've got to be right at the top of the ladder to do it. They don't employ an ordinary worker, or a Team Leader come to that. They wouldn't have them back as a consultant. You've got to be either a Managing Director or somebody, a head of a department or somebody like that." (R145, male employed manual worker, HEALTH PRODUCTS)

Attitudes to downsizing

None of the three case study organisations had specific policies allowing employees to downshift in the period before retirement, although LOCALGOV was in the process of investigating and piloting such a scheme. Most of the retired and employees who were interviewed had never particularly thought about downshifting but when the idea was introduced it received widespread support:

"Yes, I think that would be a great idea for people who are contemplating retirement early or before 65 because that's been brought up quite a few times to try and cut down their hours so they can get sort of used to slowly getting into semi-retirement and retirement." (R11, male manual employee retired, LOCALGOV)

"But I always thought it was suddenly one day you're there and the next day you're not, it's a bit of a harsh termination and I think for a lot of people a tapered situation would be much better." (R135, male manager retired, HEALTH PRODUCTS)

"I think from my point of view what would be an option would be perhaps to introduce a scheme where if you so desired you could have a stepped retirement. In other words you could ... perhaps over a period of two or three years you could reduce your working week from the normal five days to perhaps four days to perhaps three days, which has the effect of not doing away with your experience that you've accumulated in the job over all those years, you're retained to that point of view and therefore hopefully have an input into your experience in doing your job which will ultimately benefit the company but also it helps you ease in to retirement as well, rather than coming in and doing a normal week, finish on a Friday and that's it. The end." (R171, female white-collar employee, HEALTH PRODUCTS)

However, it is true to say that not everyone felt like this:

"I'd rather keep running to the end and then jump off the cliff." (R70, male manager retired, TRANSPORT)

"No, I wouldn't consider it [downshifting] at the moment. I'd rather retire once and for all, and do something different." (R101, female white-collar employee, TRANSPORT)

Downshifting within the current employment may raise issues of status for the individual or possibly the need to accept lower wages (House of Lords, 2003, p 23), both of which may be unpalatable. Among our respondents there was a minority who expressed such a view, but nevertheless it suggests that downshifting will not be attractive to everyone, although most consider it is a good idea in principle:

"Do you think it would be a good idea to reduce your hours before you go or do you think …?"

"Yes. I would have thought it would be an excellent idea and if anyone has got to go to 65 to start reducing it at 60 as a sort of a run in. But I don't think I … I personally couldn't have done that. I couldn't have had someone come in over me and I'd be his assistant." (R48, male manager retired, LOCALGOV)

"But it wasn't in our culture and for me personally if I'd started doing that [downshifting] I would have felt I was being put on the outside a bit. Myself I would have felt I was being away from the centre of what was going on in my department and what I wanted to do and I was being sidelined a bit and I wouldn't have liked that, but that's me personally." (R70, male manager retired, TRANSPORT)

Some respondents felt that the nature of their jobs would make it difficult to reduce hours or change roles. There was also a significant group who felt they simply could not afford to work less in the run-up to full retirement. However, the most commonly expressed barrier to downshifting was perceived to be the pension penalty of reducing hours in a final salary scheme. Here, the lack of understanding of pensions reported in Chapter 3 played a crucial role. A lot of people simply had no idea what effect a reduction in hours or a change in roles would have on their pensions:

"I mean a new person might prefer to just come in and have a completely clean sheet

but I've been there 50 years now really so if you had somebody working with you, you reduced your hours and they came in. I can see there'd be some sense there but goodness knows what would happen to your pension." (R43, female white-collar employee, LOCALGOV)

"And I think you start dropping on your pension as well because if you drop your income pay you drop your pension pay." (R113, male manual employee, TRANSPORT)

Downshifting to a less well paid job is likely to have consequences for pensions in a final salary scheme, a factor that was found to be a constraint in a study of older nurses (Watson et al, 2003, p 19). However, the same study identified creative responses to this problem in at least one healthcare trust. In our study there was particular confusion over the effects that moving to part-time work would have on the pension:

"I think that is the irritant really at the moment, probably with most people, that in order to keep the final salary pension scheme you can't really do part-time working because you'll miss out on your pension whereas probably the older you get it would be quite nice to have the extra day off a week because I do find working five days a week hardgoing sometimes." (R55, female employed manager, LOCALGOV)

"I have often thought about this [reducing hours] and I think the opportunity would be there if I wanted to but I'm in a final salary scheme so it's just not on." (R85, female white-collar employee, TRANSPORT)

"I don't think it would work for me because of the effect it would have on my pension. If I do less hours and that." (R104, male manual employee, TRANSPORT)

This confusion over pension composition and entitlements compounds the difficulties of considering the financial aspects of downshifting, as people often did not understand what the implications of reducing their workload would be. Many people like those just quoted did not understand that if they reduced their hours it would have an effect on the numbers of years that their pension was calculated over rather than the amount of their final salary. It was a common misapprehension that working reduced hours would have a dramatic effect on pension entitlement. In general people were unclear about the different effects that various downshifting options might have.

There were a number of examples of people in HEALTH PRODUCTS who had negotiated a variation in hours or roles prior to retirement and were generally pleased with the result:

"Yes, as I told you before I was going to retire and then when I came onto days it was a totally different role and I was quite happy and I think that if you can somehow give people that job satisfaction they will stay on. Remove the pressures and things and let them slow down." (R167, male manual employee, HEALTH PRODUCTS)

"I've been talking to [T] who is my boss and we've decided that as of next April when I shall be reached the grand old age of 62 I shall start working less hours. We're thinking about cutting it to four days a week.... So that was the idea that I would slowly cut down and expose new people to the work and oversee them until they're confident to pick it up." (R174, male manager, HEALTH PRODUCTS)

"Last year I was working full-time and my husband was still working here then as well. I knew he was going to think about retiring and I didn't want to be full-time while he was at home and also I found the job was getting too demanding and I was getting too tired and also I've got elderly parents who were taking up a lot of my time at the weekends and so I approached my manager about doing less hours, which from August I did. I only came in four days a week from August. So I reduced my time from August. My husband retired at Christmas so from Christmas I am working three days a week until I retire." (R141, female white-collar employee, HEALTH PRODUCTS)

There was also some support for the idea of flexible or gradual retirement, although the concept was largely unknown:

"I mean that would be great. I mean I would probably quite happily work until I was 61 if the hours were halved. But you see drawing your pension and halving your hours would be brilliant. I mean the other option would be to go out self-employed. I mean there's enough work kicking around this area to keep you busy." (R106, male manual employee, TRANSPORT)

Summary

From our case studies there was broad support from managers and employees for the idea of allowing people to downshift prior to retirement, even from those who personally felt they would not want to do it. There was some interest in 'flexible retirement' – that is, the possibility of drawing some pension while continuing to work but with reduced hours. There is also limited evidence to suggest that there may be a move away from the typical pattern of older workers leaving their career employer to move on to lower skilled, less well paid employment in the external labour market. In LOCALGOV and TRANSPORT there were increasing opportunities to 'come back' into other roles or on different contracts after retirement. However, as with most other decisions in the retirement zone, discretion over such opportunities was firmly in management's hands.

Although there were not explicit policies in place in the organisations studied, in practice most of those interviewed felt there was scope to ask for a reduction in hours or change of roles if they wanted to. There were also good examples of people having achieved a downshift. However, the main constraints mentioned by respondents were their current financial situation and/or the effect of reduced hours on their pensions. Current discussions about flexible or gradual retirement, in which employees could continue working while drawing some of their occupational pension (DWP, 2002, p 8), would meet with approval from employees and might serve to keep some people in work for longer, albeit on reduced hours. However, the ability to take up such flexibility might be firmly rooted in individual financial circumstances: as we have seen throughout, there is a major distinction to be made between those who might want to continue working out of interest and those who feel they must carry on working to sustain

income. Perhaps more significant is the effect
poor understanding of pensions has on
individuals' ability to think through the
implications that different downshifting options
might have. Once again, we have found that
there is a profound need for a better
understanding of pensions and retirement
options.

6

Conclusions

In this conclusion we seek to do three things:

- summarise the research findings as discussed in the preceding chapters;
- bring the findings together to explore how organisational policies and practice interact with individual dispositions and preferences to produce the dynamics of retirement decisions;
- draw out the policy implications of the research findings.

Research findings

Lost opportunities, inefficiencies and inequalities in the way that the retirement process is currently managed

Our exploration of the application of retirement policies in the three case study organisations leads to the conclusion that employers/ organisations have hitherto rarely seen the management of retirement and pensions as a tool for achieving broader or more strategic human resource goals. What happens in this area is typically driven by commercial or organisational pressures arising from other business objectives, such as reducing headcount to save money, and restructuring following takeovers, mergers and acquisitions. Hence, the operation of management discretion over retirement timing is often experienced by individual employees as arbitrary and unfair. This ad hoc approach to the management of older workers can also lead to unintended consequences for the organisation: the loss of skills and experience that may then need to be bought back in on consultancy rates; the apparently perverse reward of early retirement given to poor performers with the resulting demotivation of those who remain; the

failure to make employees fully aware of the benefits of the pension arrangements they belong to impacting on recruitment and retention.

However, there was also evidence of change in practice. The era of mass early retirements with enhanced pensions was generally felt by both managers and employees to have ended. Nevertheless organisations wished to retain their power to use early retirement as a tool as and when they deemed necessary. There were also discussions going on in all three organisations about the likely impact of age discrimination legislation and in LOCALGOV some consideration of the potential benefits of extending opportunities for downshifting prior to full retirement. It could not be said, however, that there was much sense of a step change in how the organisations viewed older workers. The tightening up of early and ill-health retirement provisions and discussions about raising the age at which employees could request early retirement were largely driven by commercial pressures and appeared to be largely financially determined. This leaves open the very real possibility that the management of older workers remains tied to short-term responses to prevailing economic conditions and that a return to previous commercial circumstances could bring a return to earlier practices.

Lack of knowledge and understanding of pension policies and retirement

We found widespread confusion among employees and the retired about how pensions were calculated and a tendency among the employed to delay getting detailed information on their own pension situations. This was despite the fact that they all worked for organisations that provided good information on demand about such matters and issued annual statements on individual pension status. Many people were simply not interested in pension details. They found them difficult or depressing to consider. Our conclusion is that it is not enough to provide information on demand. People may not demand it soon enough to be able to make sensible plans and decisions about their financial futures. Better financial education and understanding, not just information, is thus critical.

The human tendency to sharply discount the effects of present behaviour on future circumstances remains a constant. Furthermore even when information is provided people may not have the financial literacy to be able to understand it. The quality of advice may be poor. A number of respondents who had faced decisions about whether or how to move pension entitlements from previous employment had suffered from inadequate or poor guidance; they needed greater understanding of pension and investment issues to be able to make a critical assessment of the advice they were being given.

The already-retired in our study came to see, in retrospect, the need to get information and advice earlier. All three of the case study organisations made provision to send pre-retirees on courses giving advice about how to plan and manage their retirements, not only from a financial point of view but also in respect of social and health needs. These pre-retirement courses were generally seen as helpful and occasionally useful but as having occurred too late.

The desire for more choice about when to retire

It is perhaps not surprising that the overwhelming majority of respondents felt that there should be more individual choice about when to retire, either in respect of going early or being allowed to work beyond normal retirement age for their job. However, the numbers of involuntary early retired among our respondents were small, suggesting that this form of forced early retirement, for the moment at least, is in decline. Conversely, there was a considerable number of people across all three organisations

who felt forced to retire because they had reached the normal retirement age. Normal retirement ages were generally felt to be arbitrary and unfair, even by those who had or planned to retire early. There would be considerable public support for their removal, especially from lower paid workers who may otherwise, like many of the TRANSPORT employees, be forced to retire some time before they are entitled to the state pension.

From the individual experiences of our respondents we saw how individual factors such as financial position, domestic circumstances, work satisfaction, health status and the pull of the 'other non-work life' came together in the 'retirement zone' to condition the individual's aspirations and preferences about when and how to retire. However, the context in which these factors played a role was that of organisational policy and more importantly organisational practice. Management discretion over early retirement initiated by the employee or by the organisation, over whether people could continue to work in some fashion beyond normal retirement age, or over opportunities for downshifting in the run-up to full retirement, all form the context in which the individual seeks to manage their own retirement. As we see from individual accounts over and over again, the outcomes are highly contingent, often unpredictable and frequently beyond the individual's control. More senior employees are likely to be in a stronger position to bargain with the organisation for a mutually satisfactory outcome. Many lower grade staff must simply deal with what is, or is not, offered to them.

The overall conclusion is that the retirement experience has been individualised both culturally and in practice. Where in the past people would expect to continue working to normal retirement age, barring redundancy or major health problems, now there are more possibilities, but individuals' choices among these possibilities are in most cases profoundly constrained. In this sense many of the risks of retirement have been effectively privatised to the individual. In response to weak public pension provision and considerable management discretion over the timing and manner of retirement, individuals are forced to construct their own strategies, sometimes with little prior knowledge or understanding of their pension position. As a result a recurrent theme among our retired respondents and some employees was the feeling that they had somehow mismanaged their choices or that luck had not been on their side.

Support for downshifting work prior to full retirement

There was broad support from managers and employees for the principle of downshifting both work hours and roles prior to full retirement, where people wished to do so. In a sense this is an idea whose time has come. However, people's abilities to take up offers were they available will always be severely constrained by their financial situations. Among lower paid employees in our organisations, downshifting was often seen as a good idea but not one they could afford to contemplate where full-time work remained an option. However, it might be financially more attractive than full retirement, particularly if employees are allowed to draw some pension while continuing to work reduced hours, as is presently being considered by government.

A major block to thinking about downshifting was people's confusion or misunderstanding about the implications it might have for their pensions. Many simply had not thought about it and off the top of their heads could not guess what the implications might be for their pensions. A not uncommon misunderstanding was that moving to part-time hours would have a seriously detrimental effect on pension entitlement to an extent that was not the case. This is a further example of how a lack of understanding about pensions seriously inhibits people's capacity to think and plan ahead for retirement. For downshifting to become a popular route to full retirement, these largely unfounded fears about the impacts on pension would need to be allayed.

The dynamics of retirement decisions: happy retirement?

In this section we wish to consider the broader significance of our research findings. In particular, are current patterns of retirement optimal for any, or all, of the stakeholders, namely individuals, employers or society as a whole? As Blaikie (1997, p 21) commented in another connection, research based on the biographies of individuals "encounters the danger of producing studies of individual experiences without broader applicability". In this research we have a wealth of individual stories, aspirations and outcomes that richly demonstrate the variety and complexity of retirement decisions and transitions. However, by situating these in the context of the organisations from which these individuals have already or are most likely to retire, we go beyond the individual narrative to explore and shed light on the interplay between organisational policy and practice and individual choice. We use the concepts of the retirement zone and retirement scenarios as devices to shed light on these processes. As the individual enters the retirement zone (in our organisations from about the age of 50), a range of different retirement possibilities are encountered. The individual brings into the retirement zone a particular set of individual circumstances and dispositions, in terms of health, finances, job satisfaction and non-work life interests. These are not fixed but may change according to personal, family or organisational dynamics. In the retirement zone the individual also faces specific organisational pressures, encouragements or discouragements to take early retirement, and the presence or absence of the opportunity to continue work beyond normal retirement age. Many of these are factors that the individual may have little control over. In our organisations it could not be said that there was a consistent retirement process or a corporately constructed strategy for managing retirements. Organisational policy was more a function of prevailing business or budget conditions, which might even be section based rather than affecting the whole firm. The exit of older workers from the organisations was not actively managed as a whole but rather responded to in a piecemeal way according to immediate pressures mediated by flexible custom and practice.

Placed in these organisational constraints, but sharing cultural conventions about the opportunities of life in the third age, individuals wish to construct their own plans for retirement. But they do so with poor understanding of the realities of their pension situation. The effect of this interplay of organisational power and individual dispositions may frequently be suboptimal for everyone. There are real clashes of interest here. The individual may wish to retire but the organisation is reluctant to lose them; the individual may want to work on but the organisation is keen to 'refresh' the post with a younger (and probably cheaper) alternative. As in any aspect of employment relations there are conflicts of interest and the employing organisation usually has the balance of power to determine outcomes.

This suggests that both from an individual and an organisational perspective, retirement is often not well managed. From a societal perspective, this obviously raises problems too. Government fears the worsening dependency ratio as the numbers in employment shrink and those inactive or retired increase and policy is increasingly focused on what it sees as the twin problems of the labour market withdrawal of older workers and the weakness of their savings for older age. However, in both popular and policy discussions there is often a fundamental misconception of retirement behaviour: namely, that for the majority of people it is an individual decision-making process. The language of choice, 'taking' early retirement, reinforces this, as do current government policy documents, which argue:

> Individuals need to be able to plan for their retirement and make real and informed choices about how and when to save and how long to work. (DWP, 2004, p 5)

Many of our respondents had tried to take personal responsibility for these issues but lacked understanding of their pensions and hence could not plan effectively, while many others preferred to work but reached normal retirement age and were forced to retire. Many individuals have accepted that planning for retirement is a personal responsibility but as yet they lack the empowerment that would make it a reality. This research has demonstrated the need to also understand and address corporate responsibility as a major factor in current retirement patterns.

Policy implications

The research findings suggest four key implications for policy as follows.

1. Attempts by governments to encourage people to work for longer must recognise that the context in which people negotiate retirement is an organisational one and they may have little personal discretion over the timing and manner of their departure from work. Urging individuals to change their behaviour will not be sufficient if organisations are not similarly encouraged to reappraise their management of older workers.

2. Simply providing information about pensions, either on demand or regularly, is not sufficient if people do not understand the information or advice that they receive. Our findings strongly support current policy initiatives to improve the financial literacy of people from as early an age as possible.

3. This research suggests that there would be considerable popular support for the abolition of normal retirement ages within organisations. These currently act as a constraint on individuals who would like to continue working and are generally seen as arbitrary and unfair.

4. Within the organisations and among our respondents there was considerable interest in, and support for, ideas about ways of downshifting workload in the run-up to retirement. These included support for the idea of a flexible retirement, which allowed people to draw some pension while continuing to work. However, the implications of downshifting for pension entitlements need to be much more transparent.

References

Alcock, P., Beatty, C., Fothergill, S., Macmillan, R. and Yeandle, S. (2003) *Work to welfare: How men become detached from the labour market*, Cambridge: Cambridge University Press.

Anderson, M., Yoajun, L., Bechhofer, F., McCrone, D. and Stewart, R. (2000) 'Sooner rather than later? Younger and middle-aged adults preparing for retirement', *Ageing and Society*, vol 20, pp 445-66.

Arthur, S. (2003) *Money, choice and control: The financial circumstances of early retirement*, Bristol: The Policy Press/Joseph Rowntree Foundation.

Audit Commission (1997) *Retiring nature: Early retirement in local government*, London: Audit Commission.

Bardasi, E. and Jenkins, S.P. (2002) *Income in later life: Work history matters*, Bristol: The Policy Press/Joseph Rowntree Foundation.

Bardasi, E., Jenkins, S.P. and Rigg, J.A. (2000) *Retirement and the economic well-being of the elderly: A British perspective*, working paper, Essex: University of Essex, Institute for Social and Economic Research.

Beatty, C. and Fothergill, S. (2003a) 'The over 50s', in P. Alcock, C. Beatty, S. Fothergill, R. Macmillan and S. Yeandle (eds) *Work to welfare: How men become detached from the labour market*, Cambridge: Cambridge University Press.

Beatty, C. and Fothergill, S. (2003b) 'Evidence to the House of Lords Select Committee on Economic Affairs', in House of Lords Select on Committee Economic Affairs *Aspects of the economics of an ageing population*, vol 2, London: HMSO.

Beehr, T.A. (1986) 'The process of retirement: a review and recommendations for future investigation', *Personnel Psychology*, vol 39, pp 31-56.

Blaikie, A. (1997) 'Age consciousness and modernity: the social reconstruction of retirement', *Self, Agency and Society*, vol 1, no 1, pp 9-26.

Blundell, R., Meghir, C. and Smith, S. (2002) 'Pension incentives and the pattern of early retirement', *The Economic Journal*, vol 112 (March), pp C153-C170.

Bonoli, G. (2000) *The politics of pension reform*, Cambridge: Cambridge University Press.

Bryman, A. (2001) *Social research methods*, Oxford: Oxford University Press.

Campbell, N. (1999) *Decline of employment among older people in Britain*, Centre for Analysis of Social Exclusion paper 19, London: London School of Economics and Political Science.

Dench, S. and Norton, R. (1996) *Leaving employment early*, report no 322, Brighton: Institute for Employment Studies.

DfEE (Department of Education and Employment) (2000) *Factors affecting retirement. Book 1: Introduction, overview and conclusions*, Nottingham: DfEE.

Disney, R. and Hawkes, D. (2003) 'Why has employment recently risen among older workers in Britain?', in R. Dickens, P. Gregg and J. Wadsworth (eds) *The labour market under New Labour*, Basingstoke: Palgrave/Macmillan.

Disney, R., Grundy, E. and Johnson, P. (eds) (1997) *The dynamics of retirement*, Department of Social Security report no 72, London: HMSO.

DWP (Department for Work and Pensions) (2002) *Simplicity, security and choice: Working and saving for retirement*, Cm 5677, London: HMSO.

DWP (2003) *Factors affecting the labour market participation of older workers*, London: HMSO.

DWP (2004) *Simplicity, security and choice: Informed choices for working and saving*, Cm 6111, London: HMSO.

Evason, E. and Spence, L. (2003) 'Women and pensions: time for a rethink', *Social Policy and Administration*, vol 37, no 3, pp 253-70.

Evason, E., Dowds, L. and Devine, P. (2002) 'Pensioners and the Minimum Income Guarantee: observations from recent research', *Social Policy and Administration*, vol 36, no 1, pp 36-45.

Ginn, J., Street, D. and Arber, S. (2001) *Women, work and pensions: International issues and prospects*, Buckingham: Open University Press.

Gregg, P. and Wadsworth, J. (1998) 'Unemployment and non-employment: unpacking economic activity', *Economic Report*, vol 12, no 6, London: Employment Policy Institute.

Guillemard, A.-M. (1997) 'Re-writing social policy and changes within the life course organisation. A European perspective', *Canadian Journal on Aging*, vol 16, no 3, pp 441-64.

Hayden, C., Boaz, A. and Taylor, F. (1999) *Attitudes and aspirations of older people: A qualitative study*, Department of Social Security research report 102, London: HMSO.

House of Lords (2003) *Aspects of the economics of an ageing population*, vol 1 report. HL Paper 179-I, London: HMSO.

Kohli, M. and Rein, M. (1991) 'The changing balance of work and retirement', in M. Kohli, M. Rein, A.-M. Guillemard and H. Van Gunsteren (eds) *Time for retirement*, Cambridge: Cambridge University Press.

Lissenburgh, S. and Smeaton, D. (2003) *Employment transitions of older workers*, Bristol: The Policy Press/Joseph Rowntree Foundation.

McGoldrick, A. and Cooper, C. (1994) 'Health and ageing as factors in the retirement experience', *European Work and Organizational Psychologist*, vol 4, no 1, pp 1-20.

Mason, J. (2002) *Qualitative researching* (2nd edn), London: Sage Publications.

Maule, A.J., Cliff, D.R. and Taylor, R. (1996) 'Early retirement decisions and how they affect later quality of life', *Ageing and Society*, vol 16, pp 177-204.

Mayhew, V. (2001) *Pensions 2000: Public attitudes to pensions and planning for retirement*, DSS research no 130, Leeds: CDS.

Meghir, C. and Whitehouse, E. (1997) 'Labour market transitions and retirement of men in the UK', *Journal of Econometrics*, vol 79, pp 327-54.

Phillipson, C. (1982) *Capitalism and the construction of old age*, London: Macmillan.

Phillipson, C. (1999) 'The social construction of retirement: perspectives from critical theory and political economy', in M. Minkler and C.L. Ester (eds) *Critical gerontology*, Amityville, NY: Baywood Publishing Company.

Phillipson, C. (2002) *Transitions from work to retirement*, Bristol: The Policy Press/Joseph Rowntree Foundation.

PIU (Performance and Innovation Unit) (2000) *Winning the generation game: Improving opportunities for people aged 50-65 in work and community activity*, Cabinet Office, London: HMSO.

Tanner, S. (1998) 'The dynamics of male retirement behaviour', *Fiscal Studies*, vol 19, no 2, pp 175-96.

Taylor, P. (2002) *New policies for older workers*, Bristol: The Policy Press/Joseph Rowntree Foundation.

Vickerstaff, S., Cox, J. and Keen, L. (2003) 'Employers and the management of retirement', *Social Policy and Administration*, vol 37, no 23, pp 271-87.

Watson, R., Manthorpe, J. and Andrews, J. (2003) *Nurses over 50: Options, decisions and outcomes*, Bristol: The Policy Press/Joseph Rowntree Foundation.

Appendix:
Methodology

The organisations identified potential respondents in the three categories (retired, pre-retired and employees) by selecting them from their payroll or employer database. The sample was then selected in a purposive manner – that is, an attempt was made to match the gender profile of each organisation and to have both managerial and non-managerial staff in LOCALGOV and white-collar and manual workers in TRANSPORT and HEALTH PRODUCTS. The employees/retirees were then sent a letter inviting them to participate in the research by contacting one of the research team. This letter explained that the research was independent of the employing organisations and that they were under no obligation to take part if they did not wish to. To achieve close to the desired sample size of 40 employees and 20 ex-employees, a total of 180 letters were sent out to LOCALGOV respondents, 240 in the case of TRANSPORT and 160 in HEALTH PRODUCTS. Towards the end of the TRANSPORT case study the company underwent a significant process of restructuring and this reduced the numbers it was possible to interview. HEALTH PRODUCTS was also involved in a major business acquisition and this meant that we had to complete the interviews more quickly than had originally been intended.

The total of 160 respondents were either interviewed at work, in their own home or at the interviewer's place of work in the period May 2002-May 2003. The interviews were semi-structured and lasted, on average, between 45 minutes and one hour. This type of interview was used particularly because, as Mason (2002) points out, it can be especially useful in providing a detailed, contextual and multi-layered interpretation of a particular social problem. She goes on to say that this type of qualitative research can be revealing "because its sensitivity to context maximises the chances of developing fully meaningful points of comparison, where superficial 'measures' may be too crude" (2002, p 75). The interviews were transcribed and the data searched manually for theorised and emerging analytic themes. These were coded and then put into the qualitative data analysis software package NUD*IST QSRN6.

Table A1: Gender composition of the total sample

Organisation	Women	Men
LOCALGOV	38	22
TRANSPORT	9	39
HEALTH PRODUCTS	8	44

Table A2: Gender and status of the sample

	Employees		Close to retirement		Retired	
	M	F	M	F	M	F
LOCALGOV	7	13	4	16	11	9
TRANSPORT	14	2	9	5	16	2
HEALTH PRODUCTS	13	5	13	2	18	1
Totals	34	20	26	23	45	12

Note: M=Male; F=Female

Also available in the Transitions after 50 series
Published in association with the Joseph Rowntree Foundation

This highly topical new series of reports explores people's experiences, decisions and constraints as they pass from the active labour market participation in their middle years towards a new identity in later life. Each report looks in particular at issues relating to work, income and activities beyond work during this period of transition. This series is important reading for policy makers, academics and practitioners who have an interest in employment, pensions and retirement issues.

Crossroads after 50
Donald Hirsch
This report is an overview of the findings of all reports in the series.
Paperback £13.95 1SBN 1 85935 155 7

Money, choice and control
The financial circumstances of early retirement
Sue Arthur
Paperback £13.95 ISBN 1 86134 476 7

Nurses over 50
Options, decisions and outcomes
Roger Watson, Jill Manthorpe and JoyAnn Andrews
Paperback £11.95 ISBN 1 86134 544 5

Transitions from work to retirement
Developing a new social contract
Chris Phillipson
Paperback £11.95 ISBN 1 86134 457 0

Forging a new future
The experiences and expectations of people leaving paid work over 50
Helen Barnes, Jane Parry and Jane Lakey
Paperback £11.95 ISBN 1 86134 447 3

The pivot generation
Informal care and work and fifty
Ann Mooney, June Statham and Antonia Simon
Paperback £11.95 ISBN 1 86134 402 3

Early retirement and income in later life
Pamela Meadows
Paperback £11.95 ISBN 1 86134 442 2

Income in later life
Work history matters
Elena Bardasi and Stephen P. Jenkins
Paperback £12.95 ISBN 1 86134 401 5

New policies for older workers
Philip Taylor
Paperback £13.95 ISBN 1 86134 463 5

Employment tranistions of older workers
The role of flexible employment in labour market participation and promting job quality
Stephen Lissenburgh and Deborah Smeaton
Paperback £13.95 ISBN 1 86134 475 9

Outlawing age discrimination
Foreign lessons, UK choices
Zmira Hornstein, Sol Encel, Morley Gunderson and David Neumark
Paperback £14.95 ISBN 1 86134 354 X

For further information about these and other titles published by The Policy Press,
please visit our website at: www.policypress.org.uk or telephone +44 (0)117 331 4054

To order, please contact:
Marston Book Services
PO Box 269
Abingdon
Oxon OX14 4YN
UK Tel: +44 (0)1235 465500
Fax: +44 (0)1235 465556
E-mail: direct.orders@marston.co.uk